ULTIMATE SHOP DESIGN

teNeues

ULTIMATE
SHOP DESIGN

Editors: Llorenç Bonet Delgado

Copy editing: Cristina Doncel

Layout: Cris Tarradas Dulcet

Translations: Jane Wintle (English), Susanne Engler (German)
Marion Westerhoff (French), Donatella Talpo (Italian)

Produced by Loft Publications
www.loftpublications.com

Published by teNeues Publishing Group

teNeues Publishing Company
16 West 22nd Street, New York, NY 10010, USA
Tel.: 001-212-627-9090, Fax: 001-212-627-9511

teNeues Book Division
Kaistraße 18
40221 Düsseldorf, Germany
Tel.: 0049-(0)211-994597-0, Fax: 0049-(0)211-994597-40

teNeues Publishing UK Ltd.
P.O. Box 402
West Byfleet
KT14 7ZF, Great Britain
Tel.: 0044-1932-403509, Fax: 0044-1932-403514

teNeues France S.A.R.L.
4, rue de Valence
75005 Paris, France
Tel.: 0033-1-55 76 62 05, Fax: 0033-1-55 76 64 19

teNeues Iberica S.L.
Pso. Juan de la Encina 2–48, Urb. Club de Campo
28700 S.S.R.R., Madrid, Spain
Tel./Fax: 0034-91-65 95 876

www.teneues.com

ISBN-10: 3-8327-9058-6
ISBN-13: 978-3-8327-9058-5

© 2005 teNeues Verlag GmbH + Co. KG, Kempen

Printed in Spain

Bibliographic information published by
Die Deutsche Bibliothek. Die Deutsche Bibliothek lists
this publication in the Deutsche Nationalbibliografie;
detailed bibliographic data is available in the Internet
at http://dnb.ddb.de.

Rosario 4, Sevilla, Spain Tel. +34 954 216 517

www.custo-barcelona.com

Custo Barcelona / Sevilla

Architect: Air-projects **Photographer:** © Jordi Miralles

Air-projects designed this display with the product's exuberant nature in mind, which is set against uncluttered and well lit surroundings in which the clothes speak for themselves. The decoration does, however, claim a presence through the metal wall panels or the white cubes punctuating the free spaces.

Bei der Gestaltung berücksichtigten die Designer von Air-projects, dass das Produkt, das gezeigt werden soll, sehr auffallend und prachtvoll ist. Deshalb schuf man einen klaren und einfachen Raum, in dem sich die Kleidung aufgrund ihrer eigenen Schönheit abhebt. Dennoch ist die Gestaltung wahrnehmbar, so sind zum Beispiel die Wände mit Metalllamellen verkleidet und weiße Module organisieren den Raum.

Le design d'Air-projects tient compte de l'exubérance du produit à exposer, en créant un espace clair et simple où les vêtements ressortent en tant que tels. Toutefois, la décoration aussi gagne en présence grâce à des lamelles métalliques qui couvrent les parois ou à des modules blancs qui organisent l'espace.

El diseño de Air-projects tiene en cuenta la exhuberancia del producto que tienen que exhibir, por lo que crea un espacio claro y sencillo donde la ropa resalte por sí sola. Sin embargo, la decoración también gana en presencia gracias a las láminas metálicas que cubren las paredes o a los módulos blancos que ordenan el espacio.

Il design d'Air-projects tiene conto dell'esuberanza del prodotto che deve esporre, e crea dunque uno spazio chiaro e semplice in cui i capi spiccano da soli. Ciononostante, l'arredamento guadagna presenza grazie alle lamine di metallo che ricoprono le pareti o i moduli bianchi che ordinano lo spazio.

Doctor Dou 10, 08001 Barcelona, Spain Tel. +34 934 127 199

Ras Gallery

Architect: Jaime Salazar **Photographer:** © Alejandro Bachrach

The shelf is the pacesetter for this ambience, it turns and folds to accommodate books or other objects. The remaining spaces are kept free for architecture and design exhibitions, which change every few months.

Das Element, das den Raum ordnet, ist das Regal, das sich faltet, um verschiedene Ablageflächen zu bilden. Auf diesen sind Bücher und andere Objekte ausgestellt, wozu beide Seiten benutzt werden können. Der übrige Raum wird für Ausstellungen über Architektur und Design freigehalten, die alle paar Monate wechseln.

L'élément qui organise l'espace est une étagère qui se replie pour créer diverses niches afin d'y exposer des libres ou autres objets, utilisables des deux côtés. Le reste de l'espace est dépouillé pour accueillir des expositions d'architecture et de design qui modifient son aspect de temps à autres.

El elemento que ordena el espacio es la estantería, que se repliega para crear distintas repisas donde exponer libros u otros objetos, pudiendo utilizarse por ambos lados. El resto del espacio se mantiene despejado para poder acoger exposiciones de arquitectura y diseño, que modifican su fisonomía cada pocos meses.

L'elemento che ordina lo spazio è la scaffalatura, che si ripiega su se stessa per creare vari ripiani in cui esporre libri o altri oggetti, utilizzabile dai due lati. Il resto dello spazio rimane libero per accogliere mostre d'architettura e design, che modificano ogni pochi mesi la sua fisonomia.

1-2F AYBldg., 3-2-2 Kitaaoyama Minato-ku, Tokyo, Japan Tel. +81 03 5414 5870
www.custo-barcelona.com

Custo Barcelona / Tokyo

Architect: Tsutomu Kurokawa Photographer: © Kozo Takayama

The display window is a sample of the design concept used for this space, combining simplicity and complexity in a huge folded glass panel that creates unique luminous and visual effects.

Das Schaufenster zeigt das Konzept, das der Gestaltung dieses Shops zugrunde liegt. Einfachheit wird mit Komplexität kombiniert. Eine große gefaltete Glasplatte schafft interessante visuelle Effekte und eine einzigartige Beleuchtung.

La devanture est un exemple du concept qui préside le design de l'espace, combinant simplicité et complexité : une grande plaque de verre se replie sur elle même créant des effets visuels et lumineux uniques.

El escaparate es una muestra del concepto que rige el diseño del espacio, que combina sencillez y complejidad: una gran lámina de cristal se repliega sobre sí misma y crea unos efectos visuales y lumínicos únicos.

La vetrina è un esempio del concetto seguito dal design dello spazio, che abbina semplicità e complessità: una gran lamina di vetro si piega su se stessa creando degli effetti visivi e di luce unici.

Via Etna 252 / 254, 95100 Catania, Italy Tel. +39 093 342 5502
www.misssixty.com

Miss Sixty / Energie

Architect: Studio 63 Associati **Photographer:** © Yael Pincus

Yellow, the color associated with this brand, is present everywhere in the store: on the bottom of the showcases, on the vinyl cabinet taking up the entire rear wall, and on the central counter. The folds in the cabinet make ideal spaces to display accessories whilst creating a dynamic feel in the shop.

Die gelbe Farbe, die mit dieser Marke assoziiert wird, ist in dem gesamten Geschäft zu finden, angefangen bei den Rückwänden der Ausstellungselemente bis hin zu dem großen Möbel aus Vinyl, das die Wand im Hintergrund einnimmt. Auch am zentralen Verkaufstisch findet man Gelb. Die Lücken der Regale dienen zum Ausstellen von Accessoires und verleihen den Räumen zugleich eine gewisse Dynamik.

La couleur jaune associée à cette marque est présente dans toute la boutique, depuis le fond des présentoirs jusqu'au grand meuble de vinyle qui couvre tout le mur du fond ou au comptoir du meuble d'exposition central. Les espaces vides de l'étagère servent à exposer des accessoires tout en imprimant l'intérieur de dynamisme.

El color amarillo, asociado a esta marca, está presente en toda la tienda, desde el fondo de los expositores al gran mueble de vinilo que cubre toda la pared del fondo o al mostrador del mueble expositor central. Los huecos de las estanterías sirven para exponer los complementos y al mismo tiempo otorgan dinamismo al interior.

Il giallo abbinato a questa marca è presente in tutto il negozio, dai fondi degli espositori al gran mobile in vinile che ricopre tutta la parete di fondo, o il bancone del mobile espositore centrale. Gli spazi vuoti degli scaffali servono ad esporre gli accessori e, allo stesso tempo, conferiscono dinamismo agli interni.

Av. Constitució 138, Castelldefels, Spain

Parafarmacia

Architect: Manuel Bailo i Rosa Rull **Photographer:** © Jordi Miralles

Wavy shelves bring to mind an image of the sea, enhanced by the blue carpeting on floors and the tops of shelves. This simple strategy creates a unique, novel space which is also functional and practical both for customers and staff.

Die geschwungene Form der Regale erinnert an Wellen, was durch den blauen Teppichboden, der den Boden und den oberen Teil der Regale bedeckt, noch unterstrichen wird. Durch diese einfache Assoziation entsteht ein einzigartiger und moderner Raum, der für die Kunden und Angestellten zugleich funktionell und praktisch ist.

Les étagères ondulées recréent la forme de vagues, soulignées par le bleu de la moquette qui recouvre le sol et la partie supérieure des étagères. Cette idée simple permet de créer un espace innovant unique à la fois fonctionnel et pratique pour les clients et les employés.

Las estanterías onduladas recrean la forma de las olas, acentuada por el color azul de la moqueta que recubre el suelo y la parte superior de los estantes. Con este argumento sencillo se crea un espacio novedoso y único y, al mismo tiempo, funcional y práctico para los clientes y los trabajadores.

Gli scaffali ondulati ricreano la forma delle onde, accentuata dal blu della moquette che ricopre il pavimento e la parte superiore degli scaffali. Con questo semplice argomento si crea uno spazio innovativo ed unico, allo stesso tempo, funzionale e pratico per i clienti ed i dipendenti.

119 Hudson Street, New York, USA Tel. +1 212 226 0100
www.isseymiyake.com

Issey Miyake

Architect: G Tects LLC and Frank O. Ghery **Photographer:** © Roger Casas

Frank O. Gehry designed the "Tornado" sculpture for this 19th century factory, today Issey Miyake's main outlet in the United States. The sculpture consists of a group of crumpled metal sheets attached to the ceiling, stretching from the ground floor to the shop floor.

Frank O. Gehry entwarf die Skulptur "Tornado" für eine ehemalige Fabrik aus dem 19. Jh., in der sich heute das Hauptgeschäft von Issey Miyake in den Vereinigten Staaten befindet. Die Skulptur besteht aus einer Gruppe von Metalllamellen, die an den Decken angebracht sind und sich vom Untergeschoss bis zu dem Stockwerk, in dem sich das Geschäft befindet, falten und entfalten.

Frank O. Gehry a conçu la sculpture « Tornado » pour cette ancienne usine du XIXe siècle qui accueille actuellement la boutique principale d'Issey Miyake aux Etats Unis. La sculpture est formée par un groupe de plaques métalliques disposées sur les plafonds qui se rident et se déplient de l'étage inférieur jusqu'à l'étage de la boutique.

Frank O. Gehry diseñó la escultura "Tornado" para esta antigua fábrica del siglo XIX que acoge actualmente la tienda principal de Issey Miyake en Estados Unidos. La escultura está formada por un grupo de láminas metálicas dispuestas en los techos que se arrugan y despliegan desde el piso inferior hasta la planta de la tienda.

Frank O. Gehry ha disegnato la scultura "Tornado" per quest'antica fabbrica del XIX secolo attuale sede del negozio principale d'Issey Miyake negli Stati Uniti. La scultura è composta di un gruppo di lamine di metallo disposte sui tetti che si raggrinziscono e si estendono dal piano inferiore sino al piano del negozio.

16, Sloane Street, Knightsbridge, London SW1X 9NE, U.K. Tel. +44 20 7245 9520

www.marni.com

Marni

Architect: Sybarite **Photographer:** © Richard Davies

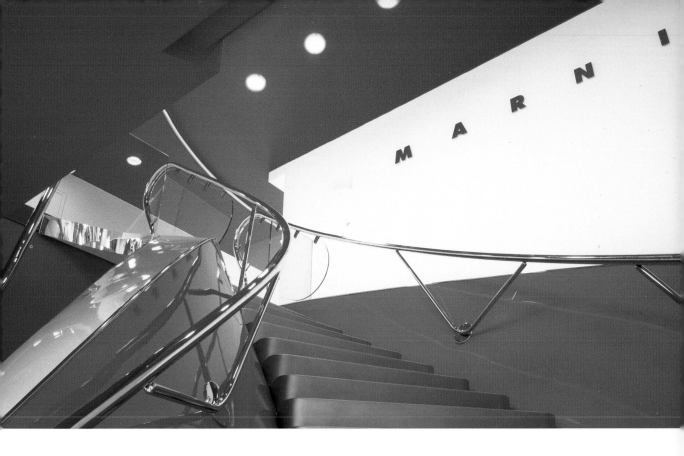

The sophisticated nature of the brand is reflected in this space where all the different elements are merged into a unique and compact design motif. The meeting point of walls and floors is rounded to create a heightened sense of continuity, and the stair handrail reaches all the way down to the floor, in a reversal of its function.

Diese edle Marke wird in einer Umgebung ausgestellt, in der alle Elemente zu einem einzigen, kompakten Design verschmelzen. Der Übergang von der Wänden zum Fußboden ist abgerundet, was ein Gefühl von Kontinuität vermittelt. Der Handlauf des Treppengeländers reicht bis zum Boden und verkehrt somit seine eigentliche Funktion.

Le caractère sophistiqué de la marque se reflète dans un espace où tous les éléments se fondent en un seul design compact. La frontière entre les murs et le sol, tout en courbes, confère la sensation de continuité, et la main courante de l'escalier parvient jusqu'au sol, invertisant sa function.

La sofisticación de la marca queda reflejada en un espacio en el que todos los elementos se funden en un sólo diseño compacto. La frontera entre paredes y suelo queda redondeada para dar sensación de continuidad, y la barandilla de la escalera llega hasta el suelo, invirtiendo su función.

La raffinatezza della marca si riflette in uno spazio in cui tutti gli elementi si fondono in un solo design compatto. La frontiera tra le pareti ed il pavimento è arrotondata per offrire una sensazione di continuità, e il corrimano della scala arriva sino a terra, tergiversando la sua funzione.

Minimalism

213, rue Saint-Honoré, 75001 Paris, France Tel. +33 1 55 35 33 90

www.colette.fr

Colette

Architect: Arnaud Montigny **Photographer:** © Roger Casas

The neutral white background of the shop creates a sensation of unity throughout the space in spite of the diverse range of its products. Each area acquires a distinctive character by means of the furniture or wall furnishings, shelves, photographs or color contrasts.

Der weiße neutrale Hintergrund des Shops lässt den ganzen Raum sehr einheitlich wirken, obwohl die verkauften Produkte sehr verschieden sind. Jeder Bereich hat durch die Möbel und Wandelemente wie durch Regale, Fotos oder die Verwendung verschiedener Farben einen eigenen Charakter.

Le fond blanc et neutre de la boutique crée une sensation d'unité dans tout l'espace, malgré la diversité de ses produits. Chaque zone possède un caractère unique grâce au mobilier ou aux éléments muraux, à l'instar des étagères, des photos ou de toute modification de couleur.

El blanco fondo neutro de la tienda permite crear una sensación de unidad en todo el espacio, a pesar de la diversidad de sus productos. Cada zona adquiere un rasgo distintivo a través del mobiliario o de los elementos de la pared, ya sean estanterías, fotos o algún cambio de color.

Il fondo neutro bianco del negozio consente di creare una sensazione d'unità in tutto lo spazio, nonostante la diversità dei suoi prodotti. Ogni zona acquisisce un aspetto diverso mediante i mobili o gli elementi della parete, siano essi scaffalature, foto o un cambio di colore.

LINEA
A MODULAR COLLECTION
GROUNDED ON BASIC
SELECTION PRINCIPLES:
LIGHT / MEDIUM / HEAVY
WEIGHT AND LIGHT /
MEDIUM / DARK TONE.
A DISPLAY INSTALLATION -
THAT DEFINES A SEQUENCE
AND A DIRECTION.

8001 Melrose Avenue, Los Angeles, CA 90046, USA Tel. +1 323 655 8160

www.costumenational.com

Costume National

Architect: Marmol Radziner and Associates **Photographer:** © Benny Chan

The high ceiling gives this shop interior a sense of weightlessness which is further increased by shades of white and indirect lighting effects through the use of spotlights hidden behind hangers. The floor-to-ceiling shelves across the walls pay homage to the minimalist sculptor Donald Judd.

Die Höhe des Ladenlokals lässt die Räume schwerelos wirken. Dieser Effekt wird durch abschattiertes Weiß und die indirekte Beleuchtung mit Spotlights, die zwischen den Aufhängevorrichtungen für die Kleidung verborgen sind, noch verstärkt. Die Regale an den Wänden reichen vom Boden bis zur Decke. Sie sind eine Hommage an den minimalistischen Bildhauer Donald Judd.

La hauteur de la boutique dégage une sensation d'apesanteur accentuée par les couleurs blanches et la lumière indirecte dont les foyers sont cachés derrière les porte-manteaux des vêtements. Les étagè-res qui recouvrent les murs du sol au plafond sont un hommage évident au sculpteur minimaliste Donald Judd.

La altura de la tienda proporciona una sensación de ingravidez acentuada por los colores blancos y la luz indirecta, con los focos escondidos tras los colgadores de la ropa. Las estanterías que recorren los muros desde el suelo hasta el techo son un claro homenaje al escultor minimalista Donald Judd.

L'altezza del negozio offre una sensazione di leggerezza accentuata dal color bianco e dalla luce indi-retta, con spot nascosti dietro gli appendi abiti. Gli scaffali che coprono i muri dal pavimento sino al tetto sono un chiaro omaggio allo scultore minimalista Donald Judd.

47, rue des Francs-Bourgeois, 75004 Paris, France Tel. +33 1 44 54 07 05

A-POC Space

Architect: Ronan and Erwann Bouroullec **Photographer:** © Roger Casas

As the window displays are sparsely decorated, the entire shop can be seen from the street without anything obscuring its central area. The "cloud" shelves, easy to assemble on account of this shape and light weight, make it possible to change the interior layout, and without losing the uncluttered and open aspect.

Da die Schaufenster nur minimal gestaltet sind, kann man von der Straße aus den ganzen Shop über-blicken, ohne dass irgendein Element den zentralen Teil verdeckt. Die aufgrund ihrer Form und ihres geringen Gewichtes einfach zu montierenden Regale „Cloud" machen es möglich, die Aufteilung im Inneren zu verändern, ohne dass dabei das schlichte und offene Erscheinungsbild verloren geht.

Les devantures étant réduites à une expression minimaliste, la totalité de la boutique est visible de la rue sans qu'aucun élément n'en cache la partie centrale. Les étagères « cloud » faciles à monter grâce à leur forme et poids minime, permet de changer facilement la distribution intérieure sans perdre l'allure dépouillée et ouverte.

Los escaparates de esta tienda se reducen a la mínima expresión, y por lo tanto el interior se puede ver desde la calle sin que ningún elemento tape su parte central. Las estanterías "cloud", fáciles de montar por su forma y mínimo peso, posibilitan cambiar la distribución del interior sin perder la pre-sencia desnuda y abierta.

Grazie al fatto che le vetrine sono ridotte alla minima espressione, quasi tutto il negozio è visibile dalla strada senza che nessun elemento copra la sua parte centrale. Le scaffalature "cloud" facili da mon-tare per la loro forma ed il minimo peso, consentono di cambiare la disposizione interna senza per-dere la presenza nuda ed aperta.

2-5-1 Yurakucho, Chiyoda-ku, Tokyo, Japan

m.i.d. Shop

Architect: Fumita Design Office **Photographer:** © Nacàsa & Partners

m, i, d, shop

The materials used in this shop create a mild and pleasant atmosphere, without any direct light sources. Matt finishes on metal shelves and walls, diffused lighting and frosted glass provide a sense of calm.

Die Materialien des Shops schaffen eine sanfte und angenehme Atmosphäre, in der es keine grellen Lichtquellen gibt. Die matten Oberflächen der Regale und der metallischen Wände, die indirekte Beleuchtung und das satinierte Glas lassen das Geschäft schlicht und ruhig wirken.

Les matériaux de la boutique contribuent à créer une atmosphère douce et agréable, où il n'y a aucune source de lumière dure. Les finitions mates des étagères et des murs métalliques, les lumières indirectes et les verres glacés confèrent à la boutique sérénité et tranquillité.

Los materiales de la tienda ayudan a crear una atmósfera suave y agradable, donde no hay ningún foco de luz dura. Los acabados mates de las estanterías y paredes metálicas, las luces indirectas y los cristales glaseados consiguen imprimir serenidad y tranquilidad a la tienda.

I materiali del negozio aiutano a creare un'atmosfera soave e gradevole, in cui non appare nessun punto di luce dura. Le rifiniture opache degli scaffali e delle pareti metalliche, le luci indirette ed i vetri satinati riescono ad imprimere serenità e tranquillità al negozio.

26 Clarence Street, Kingston upon Thames, Surrey KT1 1NU, U.K. Tel +44 20 8549 9933
www.marksandspencer.com

Marks & Spencer

Architect: John Pawson **Photographer:** © Richard Davies

The idea in the case of this shop was to build a two-storey house within the brand's large department store, so that the furniture department occupies a totally separate section. The customer literally enters a house to view the furniture and design solutions proposed by the team handling these items at the store.

Planungsziel bei der Gestaltung dieses Shops war es, innerhalb eines großen Kaufhauses der Marke ein zweistöckiges Haus zu errichten, so dass die Möbelabteilung völlig vom Rest des Geschäftes isoliert ist. Der Kunde betritt ein Haus im Sinne des Wortes, um sich die Möbel und Designlösungen anzuschauen, die das Team der Marke anbietet.

La conception de cette boutique prévoit la construction d'une maison de deux étages à l'intérieur d'un grand entrepôt de l'enseigne, afin que le département du mobilier reste entièrement séparé du reste de la boutique. Le client entre littéralement dans une maison pour voir le mobilier et les solutions de design offertes par l'équipe du magasin.

El planteamiento de esta tienda es construir una casa de dos pisos dentro de un gran almacén de la marca, de manera que la sección de mobiliario queda separada totalmente del resto de la tienda. El cliente entra literalmente en una casa para ver el mobiliario y las soluciones de diseño que ofrece el equipo de la tienda.

Il concetto di questo negozio vuole costruire una casa a due piani dentro un gran magazzino della marca, in modo che il reparto mobili rimane completamente separato dal resto del negozio. Il cliente entra letteralmente in una casa per vedere i mobili e le soluzioni di design offerti dal team del negozio.

Consell de Cent 314-316, 08007 Barcelona, Spain Tel. +34 934 871 667
www.antonio-pernas.es

Antonio Pernas

Architect: Iago Seara Photographer: © Eugeni Pons

The preservation of previously existing elements is integrated in the shop's simple lines transmitting the notion of quality and simplicity this brand embodies. Despite its three-tier layout, this space acts as a unit, thanks to the open spaces around the stairs.

Existierende Elemente wurden erhalten und in die einfachen Linien des Geschäftslokals integriert. So entsteht eine Atmosphäre von Qualität und Einfachheit, die der Marke entspricht, die vorgestellt wird. Obwohl der Raum drei Ebenen hat, wirkt er als Einheit. Dies erreichte man durch Öffnungen um die Treppe.

Les éléments préexistants conservés s'intègrent aux lignes simples de la boutique et transmettent la même notion de simplicité que la marque qu'ils représentent. Répartis sur trois niveaux, l'espace est ressenti comme une unité grâce aux ouvertures disposées autour de l'escalier.

La conservación de los elementos preexistentes se integra en las líneas simples de la tienda y transmiten la misma noción de calidad y sencillez que la marca a la que representa. A pesar de sus tres niveles, el espacio se entiende como una unidad gracias a las aberturas dispuestas alrededor de la escalera.

La conservazione degli elementi preesistenti si integra nelle linee semplici del negozio trasmettendo la stessa nozione di calore e semplicità della marca che rappresenta. Nonostante i sui tre livelli, lo spazio si estende come un'unità grazie alle aperture disposte intorno alla scala.

126-127 New Bond Street, W1S 1DY, London, U.K. Tel.+ 44 20 7491 4484

Jigsaw

Architect: John Pawson **Photographer:** © John Edward Linden

The embedded spotlights arranged in lines between the walls and the ceiling fill the whole interior with a dramatic lightness, which is accentuated by the tall ceilings and the absence of hanging lamps.

Die in Wände und Decke eingelassenen und linear angeordneten Strahler lassen eine leichte Atmosphäre im gesamten Shop entstehen, die durch das Fehlen von Hängelampen und die große Höhe der einzelnen Stockwerke noch unterstrichen wird.

Les lignes de lumière encastrées entre les murs et le plafond créent une atmosphère de légèreté dans toute la boutique, accentuée par l'absence de lampes suspendues et par la hauteur importante des étages.

Las líneas de luces empotradas entre las paredes y el techo crean un ambiente de ligereza en toda la tienda, acentuado por la ausencia de lámparas colgantes y por la gran altura de los pisos.

Le linee di luci incassate nelle pareti e nel tetto creano un'atmosfera di leggerezza in tutto il negozio, accentuato dall'assenza di lampade appese e dalla grand'altezza dei piani.

Rotherstraße 16, 10245 Berlin, Germany Tel. +49 30 72 39 70
www.zumtobelstaff.com

Zumtobel Staff

Architect: Sauerbruch & Hutton Photographer: © Biter and Bredt

Light is the main protagonist in this interior, reminiscent of the original users of the building: lighting fixtures manufacturers. Daylight and artificial lighting is tinted and filtered through colored glass transforming the shop's appearance from daytime to the night.

Das Licht ist der Hauptdarsteller in diesen Räumen, die noch an die ursprüngliche Nutzung des Gebäudes als Lampenfabrik erinnern. Mithilfe von Glas in verschiedenen Farben wird sowohl das Tageslicht als auch das künstliche Licht gedämpft, so dass sich das Aussehen des Interieurs tagsüber und nachts völlig verändert.

La lumière est le protagoniste de cet espace en souvenir de la fonction d'origine de l'édifice, à savoir une usine de lampes. A cet effet, on a cherché à nuancer avec des verres de couleurs différentes tant la lumière naturelle qu'artificielle, grâce à laquelle l'intérieur change totalement d'aspect durant le jour et la nuit.

La luz es la protagonista de este espacio en recuerdo al uso original del edificio, que era una fábrica de lámparas. Para ello se ha buscado matizar con distintos vidrios de colores tanto la luz natural como la artificial, gracias a lo cual el interior cambia totalmente de aspecto durante el día y durante la noche.

La luce è la protagonista di questo spazio in ricordo dell'uso originale dell'edificio, che era una fabbrica di lampade. Pertanto si è cercato di sfumare con vari vetri colorati tanto la luce naturale quanto quella artificiale, grazie a ciò l'interno cambia totalmente aspetto durante il giorno e durante la notte.

Verner Panton

Plaza Comercial 5, 08003 Barcelona, Spain Tel. +34 932 687 219

www.vitra.com

Vitra

Architect: Sevil Peach **Photographer:** © Alejandro Bachrach

The arrangement of the furniture is the key factor here, small sets are created in contrast to the architectural features available in the locale, painted a neutral white. In addition, the furniture may be viewed one item at a time, to perceive each element equally from a distance.

In diesem Möbelgeschäft ist die Art und Weise, wie die Möbel ausgestellt werden, das Schlüsselelement. Dazu wurden kleine Inszenierungen geschaffen, die zu den architektonischen Elementen des Verkaufsraumes, die in neutralem Weiß gestrichen sind, im Gegensatz stehen. Jedes Möbelstück kann auch für sich alleine betrachtet werden. Dadurch werden seine Proportionen deutlich.

Dans cette boutique, la manière d'exposer les meubles est essentielle. A cet effet, de petites mises en scènes sont créées pour contraster avec les éléments architecturaux de l'établissement, peints en blanc neutre. De même, les meubles peuvent également être vus séparément, permettant d'obtenir une image équidistante de chaque élément.

En esta tienda, la manera de exponer los muebles es un aspecto clave, y por ese motivo se han creado pequeñas escenografías que contrastan con los elementos arquitectónicos del local, pintados de un blanco neutro. Asimismo, los muebles también se pueden ver aisladamente, lo que ayuda a obtener una imagen equidistante de cada elemento.

In questo negozio, il modo di esporre i mobili è un elemento chiave, e per questo motivo, si creano delle piccole scenografie che contrastano con gli elementi architettonici del locale, dipinti in bianco neutro. Inoltre, i mobili possono essere visti anche in modo isolato, cosa che consente di ottenere un'immagine equidistante di ogni elemento.

Mestre Nicolau 12, 08021 Barcelona, Spain Tel. +34 932 405 666
www.animabcn.com

Anima

Architect: Inés Rodriguez **Photographer:** © Alejandro Bachrach

The space and volume of the room and furniture are dissolved by the use of the color white so that the cubic showcases containing the jewels are highlighted. The carefully designed pieces, however, still provide a warm and appealing atmosphere, suited to establishing a close rapport with customers.

Durch das Weiß verschwimmen in der Wahrnehmung der Raum und die Möbel des Shops, so dass die würfelförmigen Vitrinen, in denen sich die Schmuckstücke befinden, in den Vordergrund treten. Dennoch spielen auch die Möbel im eleganten Design eine große Rolle, denn sie sind einladend und schaffen eine enge Beziehung zum Kunden.

Le blanc annule toute notion d'espace et de volume des meubles de la boutique pour surtout mettre en scène les vitrines cubiques qui contiennent les bijoux. En outre, le design peaufiné des meubles donne une sensation accueillante qui facilite une relation plus étroite avec le client.

El color blanco anula toda noción de espacio y volumen de los muebles de la tienda para que el protagonismo recaiga en las vitrinas cúbicas que contienen las joyas. Aun así, el cuidado diseño de los muebles proporciona un ambiente acogedor que facilita una relación más estrecha con el cliente.

Il color bianco annulla qualsiasi nozione di spazio e volume dei mobili del negozio per far ricadere il protagonismo sulle vetrine cubiche che contengono i gioielli. Pur così, l'attento design dei mobili da una sensazione accogliente che favorisce una relazione più stretta con il cliente.

ANILLOS PLATA

Color

Yauatcha

Bellucci

Galerie Kreo

Tom Tailor

Pierre Hermé

Christian Lacroix

Michel Guillon

Jean-Paul Gaultier

ArtQuitect

15 Broadwick Street, London W1F 0DL, U.K. Tel. +44 20 7494 8888

Yauatcha

Architect: Christian Liaigre Photographer: © Roger Casas

The setting for this oriental cake shop seeks to convey opulence commencing with straight lines and a detailed, enclosed presentation, letting bluish colors from tinted glass and vinyl to the aquarium become the main agents. The wall behind the counter has a large showcase open to the street that allows natural light to come in.

Die Gestaltung dieser orientalischen Konditorei betont die Üppigkeit durch gerade Linien und eine detailreiche und zurückhaltende Präsentation. Hauptgestaltungselement sind die Blautöne, die sowohl in den getönten Gläsern und Vinylen als auch im Aquarium am Eingang zu finden sind. In der Wand hinter dem Ladentisch befindet sich ein großes Schaufenster zur Straße, durch das Tageslicht einfällt.

La décoration de cette pâtisserie orientale recherche l'exubérance à partir de lignes droites et d'une présentation contenue, tout en détails, laissant le ton bleu dominer l'espace, allant des verres teintés et des vinyles à l'aquarium qui préside l'entrée. Le mur du fond du comptoir est doté d'une grande devanture qui donne sur la rue, laissant entrer la lumière naturelle.

El escenario de esta pastelería oriental busca la exuberancia a partir de las líneas rectas y de una presentación detallista y contenida, dejando que los colores azulados, que van desde los cristales tintados y los vinilos a la pecera que preside la entrada, sean los protagonistas. En la pared del fondo, al lado del mostrador, hay un gran escaparate que da a la calle por el que entra la luz natural.

L'ambiente di questa pasticceria orientale ricerca l'esuberanza grazie alle linee rette ed una presentazione molto dettagliata e contenuta, lasciando il protagonismo ai colori bluastri, che vanno dai vetri tinti al vinile dell'acquario che presiede l'ingresso. La parete dietro al bancone presenta una gran vetrina che da sulla strada da cui entra la luce naturale.

237-241 Via della Pace, Grosseto, Italy Tel. +39 056 42777

Bellucci

Architect: Studio 63 associati **Photographer:** © Yael Pincus

Straight lines define the sobriety of this space, accentuated by white walls and dark grey floors and rear walls. However, using red in carpets, shelves and even part of the ceiling reverses this initial mood, bringing in movement and light-heartedness.

Die geraden Linien lassen den Raum schlicht erscheinen. Diese Wirkung wird durch die weißen Wände, den dunkelgrauen Fußboden und die dunkelgrauen Wände im Hintergrund noch unterstrichen. Im Gegensatz dazu entsteht jedoch durch die Farbe Rot, die in den Teppichen, an den Regalen und sogar an einer der Decken zu finden ist, eine ganz andere Stimmung, und Shop wirkt heiterer und lebhafter.

Les lignes droites impriment l'espace de sobriété, une qualité sublimée par le blanc des murs et le gris sombre des sols et des murs du fond. Cependant, l'apparition de la couleur rouge des tapis, étagères et sur l'un des plafonds modifie entièrement cette perception conférant gaieté et dynamisme à la boutique.

Las líneas rectas imprimen sobriedad al espacio, una cualidad acentuada por el blanco de las paredes y el gris oscuro de los suelos y de las paredes del fondo. Sin embargo, la aparición del color rojo en alfombras, estanterías e incluso en uno de los techos modifica totalmente esta percepción y otorga alegría y vivacidad a la tienda.

Le linee rette imprimono sobrietà allo spazio, una qualità accentuata dal bianco delle pareti ed il grigio scuro dei pavimenti e delle pareti di fondo. Ma il rosso dei tappeti, scaffali, ed anche di uno dei tetti modifica totalmente questa percezione per conferire allegria e vivacità al negozio.

Galerie kre

T 01 53 60 18 42
F 01 53 60 17 58

ouverture du mardi au ve
de 14h à 19h
et le samedi de 11h à 19h
www.galeriekreo.com

Show Room   1, rue Zadkine   75013 P

22, rue Duchefdelaville, 75013 Paris, France Tel. +33 1 53 60 18 42
www.galeriekreo.com

Galerie Kreo

Architect: Combarel and Marrec **Photographer:** © Roger Casas

The interior of the gallery must be neutral and functional since the exhibitions frequently change. But this simplicity is not at odds with quality, as revealed by the translucent ceiling panels, which allow the fluorescent lighting to be discreet and free of inconvenience apertures or mountings.

Da Innere der Galerie muss neutral und funktionell sein, da die Ausstellungen sehr oft wechseln. Aber diese Einfachheit schließt eine qualitativ hochwertige Raumgestaltung nicht aus. Im Fall dieses Shops lassen lichtdurchlässige Paneele an der Decke das Licht durch und verbergen die Leuchtstoffröhren zugleich. So konnte man auf unelegante Blenden und Halterungen verzichten.

L'intérieur de la galerie doit rester neutre et fonctionnel, car les expositions se succèdent à un rythme fréquent. Mais cette simplicité n'exclut pas un intérieur de qualité, à l'instar des panneaux translucides du plafond, solution qui laisse passer la lumière des tubes fluorescents sans qu'ils se voient, éliminant ainsi les ouvertures ou les douilles peu pratiques.

El interior de la galería tiene que ser neutro y funcional, ya que las exposiciones se renuevan constantemente. Sin embargo, esta sencillez no está reñida con un interior de calidad, como lo demuestra la solución de los paneles translúcidos del techo, que dejan pasar la luz de los fluorescentes sin que éstos se vean, lo que permite prescindir de aberturas o incómodos portalámparas.

L'interno della galleria deve essere neutro e funzionale, perché le mostre cambiano spesso. Ma questa semplicità non è incompatibile con interni di qualità, come lo dimostra la soluzione dei pannelli semi trasparenti del tetto, che lasciano passare la luce dei neon senza che si vedano, potendo così prescindere da aperture o da scomode portalampade.

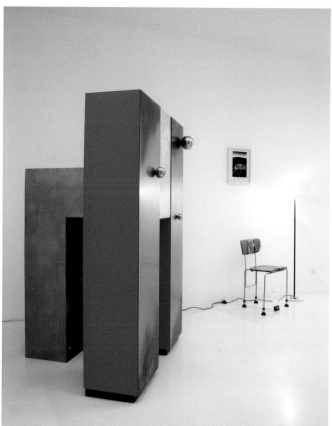

Große Bleichen 36, 20354 Hamburg, Germany Tel. +49 40 28 80 98 88
www.tom-tailor.com

Tom Tailor

Architect: Decoprojekt Photographer: © Tom Tailor

All these wide spaces allow the customer to wander comfortably through the shop. Sober lines make way for the protagonist: the product, transforming the outlet decor into a pleasurable framework for displaying apparel and accessories.

Die Weite aller Räume macht es möglich, dass die Kunden bequem durch das gesamte Geschäft schlendern können. Die schlichten Linien überlassen den ausgestellten Produkten die Hauptrolle. So wird die Dekoration dieses Geschäftes zu einem angenehmen Rahmen für die Ausstellung der Kleidungsstücke und Accessoires.

L'amplitude de tous les espaces permet au client de se promener facilement dans la boutique. Les lignes sobres donnent la part belle au produit, faisant que la décoration de la boutique se transforme en un cadre agréable pour exposer les vêtements et les accessoires.

La amplitud de todos los espacios permite que el cliente se pueda pasear cómodamente por la tienda. Las líneas sobrias ceden el protagonismo al producto, con lo que la decoración de la tienda se transforma en un agradable marco para enseñar la ropa y los complementos.

La grandezza di tutti gli spazi permette al cliente di muoversi liberamente per il negozio. Le linee sobrie cedono il protagonismo al prodotto, e l'arredamento del negozio si trasforma in un gradevole ambiente in cui esporre i capi e gli accessori.

185, rue de Vaugirard, 75015 Paris, France Tel. +33 1 47 83 89 96

Pierre Hermé

Architect: Christian Biecher **Photographer:** © Roger Casas

Monochrome surfaces, pure lines and indirect light are used to recreate an interior more reminiscent of a jeweller's than a grocer's. This strategy is also applied to labelling and packaging, and is a standard part of this French patisserie's style.

Mit den einfarbigen Oberflächen, den geraden Linien und dem indirekten Licht wurde ein Erscheinungsbild geschaffen, das eher an einen Juwelierladen erinnert als ein Lebensmittelgeschäft. Das Konzept wurde auch auf die Etiketten und Verpackungen übertragen, und bildet einen Teil des Markenimages dieser französischen Konditorei.

Avec les surfaces monochromes, les lignes droites et la lumière indirecte, on a essayé de donner une image plus proche d'une bijouterie que d'une boutique d'alimentation. Cette présentation est identique à celle des étiquettes et emballages des produits, et fait partie de l'image de marque de cette pâtisserie française.

Con las superficies monocromas, las líneas rectas y la luz indirecta se ha pretendido dar una imagen más parecida a una joyería que a una tienda de alimentos. Esta presentación es la misma que la de las etiquetas y el embalaje de los productos, y forma parte de la imagen de marca de esta pastelería francesa.

Con le superfici monocrome, le linee rette e la luce indiretta si è voluto dare un'immagine più consona ad una gioielleria che ad un negozio d'alimentari. Questa presentazione si ritrova sulle etichette e sul packaging dei prodotti, e forma parte dell'immagine di marca di questa pasticceria francese.

24-4 Saraugaku-cho, Shibuya-ku, Tokyo, Japan
www.christian-lacroix.fr

Christian Lacroix

Architect: Caps Architects **Photographer:** © Nacàsa & Partners

Colorful and translucent showcases set the pace for this interior as the sole decorative feature. As these elements are semi-transparent, the entire space can be encompassed from any angle, through the filter created by the selected range of colors.

Die farbigen und lichtdurchlässigen Ausstellungselemente sind bestimmend für die Innengestaltung des Shops und dessen einziges dekoratives Element. Da sie teilweise durchsichtig sind, kann man den Raum aus jeder Perspektive überschauen. Zugleich wirken sie wie Filter mit einer ausgewählten Farbskala.

Les présentoirs colorés et translucides donnent le ton à l'intérieur de la boutique et constituent son unique élément décoratif. Etant semi transparents, il est possible de voir tout l'espace de n'importe quel angle, au travers du filtre créé par la gamme de couleurs particulières de la boutique.

Los expositores de colores y translúcidos establecen la pauta del interior de la tienda y constituyen su único elemento decorativo. Al ser semitransparentes, es posible ver todo el espacio desde cualquier ángulo, a través del filtro creado por la particular gama de colores de la tienda.

Gli espositori colorati e traslucidi definiscono lo stile dell'interno del negozio, costituendo il suo unico elemento decorativo. Essendo semitrasparenti, consentono di vedere lo spazio da qualsiasi angolo del negozio, il tutto filtrato attraverso la particolare gamma dei colori del negozio.

35 Duke of York Square, London SW3 4LY, U.K. Tel. +44 20 7730 2142
www.michelguillon.com

Michel Guillon

Architect: Abe Rogers / KRD Photographer: © Roger Casas

This simple and attractive setting leaves the shop interior more or less empty by placing merchandise and tools of the trade in wall cabinets. Light diffused from behind the shelving displaying glasses achieves just the right amount of illumination of the product emitting a very personal corporate image.

Diese einfache und gewagte Inszenierung lässt das Innere des Shops fast leer, indem sowohl das ausgestellte Produkt als auch die Werkzeuge in den Wandschränken untergebracht sind. Die Lichtquellen befinden sich hinter den Regalen, in denen die Brillen ausgestellt werden. So wird das Produkt perfekt beleuchtet und gleichzeitig wird ein sehr persönliches Corporate Image vermittelt.

La mise en scène simple et attrayante laisse l'intérieur de la boutique presque vide, en plaçant le produit exposé ainsi que les outils dans les armoires murales. La lumière qui arrive derrière les étagères où les lunettes sont exposées, illumine le produit à la perfection, tout en transmettant une image de marque très personnelle.

Esta puesta en escena sencilla y atractiva deja el interior de la tienda casi vacío al colocar tanto el producto exhibido como los instrumentosas de trabajo en los armarios de las paredes. La luz proviene de detrás de los estantes donde se exponen las gafas, con lo que se consigue una perfecta iluminación del producto y se transmite una imagen corporativa muy personal.

Questa messa in scena semplice ed attraente lascia l'interno del negozio quasi vuoto collocando il prodotto esposto e gli strumenti da lavoro negli armadi delle pareti. La luce proviene da dietro gli scaffali dove sono esposti gli occhiali, cosa che consente di ottenere una perfetta illuminazione del prodotto e trasmette un'immagine corporativa molto personale.

44, avenue George V, 75008 Paris, France Tel. +33 1 44 43 00 44
www.jeanpaul-gaultier.com

Jean-Paul Gaultier

Architect: Philippe Starck Photographer: © Roger Casas

Shiny surfaces on the plain, linear furniture create a brilliant, luxurious interior in this shop. The mirror-clad chests of drawers and illuminated glass counters are an example of this combination of simple and complex lines as a backdrop to the creations of Jean-Paul Gaultier.

Die Linien der Möbel in diesem Shop sind gerade, doch reflektierende Oberflächen sorgen für Glanz und Pracht. Die mit Spiegeln verkleideten Schubladenschränke und die beleuchteten Verkaufstische aus Glas sind ein Beispiel für die Verbindung von Schlichtheit und komplexen Linien, die den Hintergrund abgibt für die Kleidung von Jean-Paul Gaultier.

Bien que les lignes des meubles de la boutique soient droites, la recherche de finitions miroitantes revêt l'intérieur d'éclat et de splendeur. Les armatures recouvertes de miroirs et les comptoirs de verre illuminés sont un exemple de cette alliance de simplicité et de lignes complexes, servant de toile de fond aux vêtements de Jean-Paul Gaultier.

Aunque las líneas de los muebles de la tienda son rectas, se buscaron acabados reflectantes para dar brillo y suntuosidad al interior. Las cajoneras recubiertas de espejos y los mostradores de cristal con luces son un ejemplo de esta mezcla de sencillez y líneas complejas que sirve de telón de fondo de la ropa de Jean-Paul Gaultier.

Le linee dei mobili del negozio sono rette, ma le rifiniture sono state scelte riflettenti per dare brillantezza e sontuosità agli interni. Il cassettone ricoperto di specchi, ed i banchi di vetro dotati di luci, sono un esempio di come mischiare la semplicità con le linee complesse che funge da sfondo per i capi di Jean-Paul Gaultier.

Comerç 31, 08003 Barcelona, Spain Tel. +34 932 683 096
www.artquitect.net

ArtQuitect

Architect: José Luis López Ibáñez **Photographer:** © Joan Mundó

Fluorescent light is sifted through opaque glass to produce diffuse lighting free from shadows. Movable panels, however, reveal miniature scenes requiring strong light. A striking contrast is thus formed between the product and the overall shop space.

Das Neonlicht wird durch mattes Glass gedämpft, so dass eine diffuse Beleuchtung entsteht, die Schatten und direktes Licht vermeidet. Dagegen kann man auf den beweglichen Paneelen kleine Inszenierungen sehen, bei denen eine starke Beleuchtung eingesetzt wird. So entsteht ein Kontrast zwischen dem Produkt und dem Verkaufslokal.

La lumière fluorescente tamisée au travers des verres opaques crée une luminosité diffuse qui évite les ombres et la lumière directe. Par contre, les panneaux amovibles permettent de voir des petites scénographies fortement éclairées ce qui crée un contraste entre le produit et l'espace de la boutique.

La luz fluorescente tamizada a través de cristales opacos crea una luminosidad difusa que evita las sombras y la luz directa. En cambio, los paneles móviles permiten ver pequeñas escenografías en las cuales se busca una iluminación fuerte, lo que crea un contraste entre el producto y el espacio de la tienda.

La luce fluorescente sfumata da vetri opachi crea una luminosità diffusa che evita le ombre e la luce diretta. In cambio, i pannelli mobili consentono di vedere delle piccole scenografie in cui si cerca un'illuminazione forte, che crea un contrasto tra il prodotto e lo spazio del negozio.

el guiño la despedida, ¿por q
el sueño llega a su fin, y e
en forma de luz

Renovation &
Restoration

230 Brick Lane, London E9 7EB, U.K. Tel. +44 20 7613 0882
www.untothislast.co.uk

Unto This Last

Architect: Olivier Geoffroy **Photographer:** © Roger Casas

The old storehouse where this site is located has retained its factory origins. Furthermore, a large proportion of the furniture is still manufactured on site, as can be witnessed from within one section the shop. The factory appearance contrasts with the judicious arrangement and superb design of the furniture.

Das ehemalige Lagerhaus, in dem sich der Verkaufsraum befindet, hat nicht nur seine Vergangenheit als Fabrik bewahrt sondern es werden weiterhin im gleichen Gebäude ein Großteil der Möbel hergestellt. Dies kann man in einem Bereich des Shops sehen. Das werkstattmäßige Erscheinungsbild steht zu der sorgfältigen Anordnung der Möbel und ihrem wunderschönen Design im Gegensatz.

L'ancien entrepôt qui accueille le magasin a non seulement conservé son passé industriel, mais en plus, une grande partie des meubles sont encore fabriqués dans cet édifice, comme on peut le voir à un certain endroit de la boutique. Les allures d'atelier contrastent avec la disposition très étudiée des meubles et leur design sublime.

El antiguo almacén donde se ubica la tienda no sólo ha conservado su pasado fabril sino que en el mismo edificio aún se fabrican gran parte de los muebles, como se puede ver desde una parte de la tienda. La apariencia de taller contrasta con la cuidada disposición de los muebles y con su exquisito diseño.

L'antico magazzino in cui è stato ricavato il negozio non solo non ha perso il suo passato industriale, ma addirittura nello stesso edificio si producono ancora gran parte dei mobili, come si può vedere da un lato del negozio. L'aspetto di bottega contrasta con la curata disposizione dei mobili e con il loro squisito design.

142, Galerie de Valois, Jardins du Palais Royal, 75001 Paris, France Tel. +33 1 49 27 09 09
www.salons-shiseido.com

Les Salons du Palais Royal Shisheido

Architect: Serge Lutens Photographer: © Roger Casas

The conservation of original features such as the floor, part of the furnishings, or the mid-19th century staircase gives this shop the potential to carry us back to the magnificence of a bygone era, but without this sensation overshadowing the modern elegance.

Durch die Erhaltung von Elementen, wie den Böden, einem Teil der Möbel und der Treppe, die aus der Mitte des 19. Jh. stammen, vermittelt diese Boutique den Luxus einer anderen Ära, ohne dass die elegante Atmosphäre die Modernität beeinträchtigen würde.

La rénovation d'éléments comme les sols, une partie du mobilier ou l'escalier datant de la moitié du XIXe siècle fait que cette boutique nous transpose dans le monde luxueux d'une autre époque, sans que la sensation d'élégance n'affecte la modernité de l'ensemble.

La conservación de elementos como los suelos, parte del mobiliario o la escalera de mediados del siglo XIX hace que esta tienda tenga la capacidad de transportarnos al lujo de otra época, sin que esta sensación de elegancia menoscabe la de modernidad.

La conservazione d'elementi come i pavimenti, parte dei mobili o della scala di metà del XIX secolo consente a questo negozio di trasportarci nel lusso di un'altra epoca, senza che questa sensazione d'eleganza nulla tolga a quella di modernità.

211, rue Saint Honoré, 75001 Paris, France Tel. +33 1 42 60 40 56

Chantal Thomass

Architect: Christian Ghion **Photographer:** © Roger Casas

The blinds situated behind the showcase allow natural light to permeate the interior whilst also acting as a visual screen keeping the interior space separate from the outside world. The rose tinted colors and wavy lines of the furnishings create something of a fantasy atmosphere with a touch of humor, as well as a pleasant and practical environment.

Die Bändergardine hinter dem Schaufenster lässt Tageslicht ins Innere fallen und dient gleichzeitig als Sichtschutz, so dass man von der Straße aus nicht ins Innere sehen kann. Die Rosatöne und die kurvige Linienführung der Möbel erschafft eine Phantasiewelt mit einem Quäntchen Humor und ein Ambiente, das angenehm und praktisch zugleich ist.

Le rideau de lanières situé derrière la devanture permet le passage de la lumière naturelle à l'intérieur et en même temps joue le rôle d'un tamis visuel pour éviter d'exposer l'intérieur aux regards indiscrets de la rue. Les couleurs rosées et les lignes sinueuses des meubles recréent un monde imaginaire avec une pointe d'humour et créent une ambiance agréable et pratique.

La cortina de tiras situada detrás el escaparate permite la entrada de luz natural en el interior y al mismo tiempo actúa como tamiz visual para evitar que la tienda quede expuesta a la calle. Los colores rosados y las líneas sinuosas de los muebles recrean un mundo de fantasía con un toque de humor y crean un ambiente agradable y práctico.

La tenda a strisce, situata dietro la vetrina, lascia passare la luce naturale all'interno e, allo stesso tempo, agisce come filtro visivo per evitare che l'interno sia alla mercé della strada. I colori rosati e le linee sinuose dei mobili, ricreano un mondo di fantasia con un tocco d'umore ottenendo un ambiente gradevole e pratico.

32, rue Charlot, 75003 Paris, France Tel. +33 1 42 71 45 95
www.galeriedansk.com

Galerie Dansk

Designer: Donatienne Tiberghien **Photographer:** © Roger Casas

In order to highlight the furniture to the maximum, the design for this outlet is strict simplicity, with large picture windows onto the street. The floors and walls are decorated in light colors and the sole contrasting element is the open brickwork which adds a homely touch to the ensemble.

Damit die Möbel wirklich die absolute Hauptrolle in diesem Geschäft spielen, wurde es sehr einfach gestaltet. Große Schaufenster öffnen sich zur Straße. Der Boden und die Wände sind in hellen Tönen gehalten und das einzige Element, das einen Gegensatz dazu schafft, ist die unverputzte Ziegelwand, die den Raum anheimelnd wirken lässt.

Pour que les meubles soient les grands protagonistes de l'espace, le design de la boutique est resté sobre, avec de grandes baies vitrées qui ouvrent l'intérieur vers la rue. Le sol et les murs sont clairs et l'unique élément de contraste revêt la forme d'un mur de briques apparentes créant un ensemble très chaleureux.

Para dar el máximo protagonismo a los muebles, el diseño de la tienda se basa en la sencillez, con grandes ventanales que abren el interior a la calle. El suelo y las paredes son de colores claros, y el único elemento que contrasta es un sencillo muro de ladrillo visto que otorga calidez al conjunto.

Per dare il maggior protagonismo ai mobili, il design del negozio si basa sulla semplicità, con grandi vetrate che aprono l'interno sulla strada. Il pavimento e le pareti sono di colori chiari, e l'unico elemento che contrasta è un semplice muro di mattoni a vista che da calore all'ambiente.

Herrengasse 16, Graz, Austria Tel. +43 31 680 17 96 60

Joanneum Museum Shop

Architect: Eichinger oder Knechtl **Photographer:** © Rupert Steiner

In designing this shop, the architects aimed to create a space that would stand out from the rest of the museum. So as to not interfere with the building itself, an independent structure was chosen, whose twisted walls and ceilings confer a recreational and bizarre effect.

Beim Entwurf des Geschäftes wollten die Architekten einen Raum entwerfen, der sich vom übrigen Teil des Museums abhebt. Aus diesem Grund griffen sie auf eine Struktur zurück, die das Gebäude nicht beeinträchtigt und mit ihren gewölbten Wänden und Dächern einen verspielten und ungewöhnlichen Eindruck erzeugt.

Avec cet design, les architectes voulaient créer un espace qui était différent des autres salles du musée. Pour cette raison ont utilisé une structure qui était respectueuse avec l'ancien bâtiment et présente, avec ses murs et toits penchés, un aspect ludique et étrange.

Al diseñar esta tienda, los arquitectos quisieron crear un espacio que destacara respecto al resto del museo. Por eso, recurrieron a una estructura que no perjudica el edificio y presenta, con sus paredes y techos torcidos, un aspecto lúdico y extraño.

Nel disegno di questo negozio, gli architetti hanno voluto creare uno spazio che risaltasse rispetto al resto del museo. Per questa ragione si sono avvalsi di una struttura che non pregiudica l'edificio e assume, con le pareti e i soffitti storti, un aspetto ludico e strano.

Canuda 21, 08002 Barcelona, Spain Tel. +34 933 025 281
www.leboudoir.net

Le Boudoir

Architects: Mónica Sans, Julie Plottier, Paul Reynolds **Photographer:** © Alejandro Bachrach

This quality lingerie outlet combines subtlety and cleverness in its leitmotiv, without this preventing it from using large, clear show windows. The atmosphere of a stately home is recreated with elements such as a grand fireplace, furniture or the heavy red curtains at the rear of the shop, which suggest the intimacy of the boudoir.

Die Leitmotive in dieses luxuriösen Miederwarengeschäft sind Raffinesse und Pikanterie. Ungeachtet dessen ist er durch große Schaufenster einsehbar. Der Shop ahmt die Atmosphäre einer großen Villa nach. Dazu wurden Elemente benutzt wie der Kamin, die Möbel und die große rote Gardine im hinteren Teil des Geschäftes, die einen privaten, angenehmen Raum schaffen.

Ce magasin de dessous féminin de luxe fait de la subtilité et de la friponnerie un de ses leitmotive, tout en gardant de grandes devantures transparentes. La boutique recrée l'ambiance d'une grande demeure, à l'aide d'éléments récupérés à l'instar de la cheminée, du mobilier ou du grand rideau rouge au fond de la boutique, qui crée un espace intime et accueillant.

Esta corsetería de lujo hace de la sutileza y la picardía uno de sus leitmotiv, sin que eso impida disponer de grandes escaparates transparentes. La tienda recrea el ambiente de una gran mansión, con elementos recuperados como la chimenea, el mobiliario o la gran cortina roja del fondo de la tienda, que crea un espacio íntimo y acogedor.

Questo negozio di corsetteria di lusso fa della raffinatezza e della malizia uno dei suoi leit motif, senza che ciò impedisca di disporre di grandi vetrine trasparenti. Il negozio ricrea l'ambiente di una gran dimora, con elementi recuperati come il camino, i mobili o il gran tendone rosso del fondo, che crea uno spazio intimo ed accogliente.

Ample 28, 08002 Barcelona, Spain Tel. +34 932 688 625
www.papabubble.com

Papabubble

Designer: Mr.Bones **Photographer:** © Alejandro Bachrach

This store reproduces the classical shop window common to Barcelona facades, and the shop breathes a classical air despite only being opened a few years ago. The original counters have been kept, and the original workshop where the sweets were crafted is open to view, as was customary a hundred years ago.

In diesem Shop wurde das klassische Schaufenster der Geschäfte Barcelonas erhalten. Das lässt dieses Geschäft klassisch wirken, obwohl es erst vor ein paar Jahren eröffnet wurde. Im Inneren wurde die Anordnung der Ladentische erhalten und die Konditorei, in der die Süßigkeiten hergestellt werden, ist halb offen, so wie es vor hundert Jahren der Fall war.

Cette boutique conserve la devanture classique des commerces de Barcelone, et a maintenu une aura de boutique classique malgré son ouverture relativement récente datant de quelques années seulement. A l'intérieur on a essayé de garder la structure originale des comptoirs et de laisser entrouvert l'atelier où l'on fabrique les bonbons, comme cela se faisait dans les boutiques d'antan.

Esta tienda conserva el escaparate clásico de los comercios barceloneses y ha conseguido un aura de tienda clásica a pesar de llevar abierta pocos años. En el interior se ha intentado mantener la estructura original de los mostradores y dejar entreabierto el obrador donde se elaboran los caramelos, como pasaba en las tiendas de hace cien años.

Questo negozio conserva la vetrina classica dei locali commerciali di Barcellona ed ha conquistato un'atmosfera di negozio classico pur essendo nato da pochi anni. Internamente si è cercato di mantenere la struttura originale dei banchi, lasciando semiaperto il laboratorio dove si elaborano le caramelle, come succedeva nei negozi di cent'anni fa.

Diputació 299, 08007 Barcelona, Spain Tel. +34 933 090 653

Nuevo espacio Julie Sohn

Architects: Conrado Carrasco, Carlos Tejada, Estudio CCT **Photographer:** © Alejandro Bachrach

Open brickwork makes a pleasant, neutral backdrop for apparel, and at the same time the irregular shape of the high, white ceilings make for a spacious and elegant interior. The display window on the street is a large glass pane which lets in natural daylight and reveals the two storeys inside.

Unverputzter Ziegel dient als neutraler und warmer Hintergrund, vor dem die Kleidungsstücke gezeigt werden. Die Höhe des Lokals und die unregelmäßige weiße Decke lassen den gesamten Raum weit und elegant wirken. Das Schaufenster zur Straße ist eine große Glasplatte, durch die Tageslicht auf beide Ebenen des Shops fällt.

La brique apparente sert de fond neutre et chaud pour exposer les vêtements, alors que la hauteur de la boutique et le plafond blanc irrégulier confèrent amplitude et élégance à tout l'espace. La devanture qui donne sur la rue est constituée d'une grande plaque de verre qui laisse entrer la lumière naturelle et transparaître les deux hauteurs à l'intérieur.

El ladrillo visto hace de fondo neutro y cálido en el que mostrar las prendas de ropa, mientras que la altura de la tienda y el techo blanco e irregular otorgan amplitud y elegancia a todo el espacio. El escaparate que da a la calle es una gran lámina de vidrio que proporciona luz natural y que muestra las dos alturas del interior.

Il mattone a vista che funge da sfondo neutro e caldo sul quale mostrare i capi, insieme all'altezza del negozio ed il tetto bianco irregolare, conferiscono sensazione di spazio ed eleganza a tutto l'ambiente. La vetrina che da sulla strada è una grande lamina di vetro che proporziona luce naturale e che mostra le due altezze dell'interno.

Contemporary Classic

175 Sloane Street, London SW1 X9 QG, U.K. Tel. +44 20 7201 0980
www.dolcegabbana.it

Dolce & Gabbana

Architect: David Chipperfield, Ferruccio Laviani (interiors) **Designers:** Domenico Dolce, Stefano Gabbana
Photographer: © Roger Casas

The structural elements of rectangular lines combined with dark or metallic color provide a sombre, austere background against which to display clothing and accessories. French armchairs create a dramatic contrast with the numerous restrictive lines, and the concept is more visual and sculptural than functional.

Die architektonischen Elemente mit rechteckigen Winkeln in dunklen oder metallischen Farben bilden den schlichten Hintergrund für die Kleidung und Accessoires, die in diesem karg dekoriertem Raum ausgestellt werden. Die französischen Sessel schaffen einen dramatischen Kontrast zu dieser zurückhaltenden Linienführung, deren Konzept eher visuell und skulpturell als funktionell ist.

Les éléments architecturaux des lignes rectangulaires et les couleurs sombres ou métalliques créent un fond sobre pour que les vêtements et les accessoires soient mis en relief dans cet espace si austère. Les sièges français créent un contraste dramatique devant la multitude de lignes mesurées selon un concept plus visuel et sculpté que fonctionnel.

Los elementos arquitectónicos de líneas rectangulares y colores oscuros o metálicos constituyen un fondo sobrio para que la ropa y los complementos luzcan en este espacio tan austero. Los sillones franceses crean un contrapunto dramático ante tantas líneas contenidas, y su concepto es más visual y escultórico que funcional.

Gli elementi architettonici dalle linee rettangolari e dai colori scuri o metallici, sono uno sfondo sobrio che permette ai capi ed agli accessori di brillare in questo spazio così austero. Le poltrone francesi creano un contrappunto drammatico innanzi a tante linee contenute, ed il loro concetto è più visivo e scultoreo che funzionale.

Frauenplatz 13, 80331 Munich, Germany Tel. +49 89 29 16 07 17
www.isabella-hund.de

Isabella Hund

Architect: Landau & Kindlebacher **Photographer:** © Michael Heinrich

Gold and silver are present throughout the jewelry store through the use of steel and an ingenious lighting scheme. The light colors of wooden elements provide the perfect background for displaying the jewels under warm, appealing lights.

In diesem Juweliergeschäft sind Gold- und Silbertöne aufgrund des verwendetes Stahls und der ganz besonderen Beleuchtung überall präsent. Die Holztöne der Ausstellungskästen ermöglichen es, die Schmuckstücke in einem warmen und angenehmen Licht zu präsentieren.

Les couleurs or et argent sont omniprésentes dans la bijouterie grâce à l'emploi de l'acier et à un éclairage très spécial. Le bois se décline dans une gamme de couleurs claires qui sert de cadre idéal pour exposer les bijoux sous une lumière chaude et accueillante.

Los colores dorados y plateados están presentes en toda la joyería gracias al uso del acero y a una iluminación muy especial. La madera proporciona una gama de colores clara que sirve de marco idóneo para mostrar las joyas bajo una luz cálida y acogedora.

I colori dorati e argentati sono presenti in tutta la gioielleria grazie all'uso dell'acciaio e ad un'illuminazione molto speciale. Il legno offre una gamma di colori chiara che serve da cornice idonea per mostrare le gioie sotto una luce calda ed accogliente.

21 Bruton Street, London W1J 6QD, U.K. Tel. +44 20 7629 7750
www.millerharris.com

Miller Harris

Architect: Ade Rogers / KRD **Photographer:** © Roger Casas

Reflective surfaces contribute to a rich and sumptuous interior, which in combination with the straight lines of fixtures plus the right color balance, match the elegance of the products. Within this excellent décor new life is given to the interior space even though scarcely any direct natural light is available.

Reflektierende Flächen in den Räumen schaffen ein Ambiente von Reichtum und Luxus, das durch die Geradlinigkeit der Möbel und dem gekonnten Einsatz der Farben die gleiche Eleganz vermittelt, die die Produkte besitzen. Mit dieser gelungenen Dekoration wird einem Raum Leben eingehaucht, in den fast kein Tageslicht von außen dringt.

Les intérieurs miroitants permettent de créer une ambiance riche et somptueuse qui, associée aux lignes droites des meubles et au ton de couleur juste, reflètent la même élégance que leurs produits. Cette superbe décoration donne vie à un espace intérieur qui ne reçoit pratiquement pas de lumière extérieure directe.

Los interiores reflectantes consiguen crear un ambiente de riqueza y suntuosidad que, combinado con las líneas rectas de los muebles y el punto justo de color, transmiten la misma elegancia que sus productos. Con esta excelente decoración se consigue dar vida a un espacio interior que casi no recibe luz natural directa.

Gli interni riflettenti consentono di creare un ambiente di ricchezza e sontuosità che, abbinato alle linee rette dei mobili ed il punto giusto di colore, trasmettono la stessa eleganza dei suoi prodotti. Con questo eccellente arredamento si riesce a dar vita ad uno spazio interno che quasi non riceve luce naturale.

Lagasca 50, 28001 Madrid, Spain Tel. +34 914 262 815

www.amayaarzuaga.com

Amaya Arzuaga

Architect: Francesc Pons **Photographer:** © Raimon Solà

Reminiscences of the 50's give a touch of chic to this space, with clear-cut, straight lines. The vivid lighting scheme and the reflections off metallic elements transmit a sense of extravagance to this space, where the first priority is elegance.

Die Anspielungen auf den Stil der Fünfzigerjahre lassen diesen Shop, dessen Design auf geraden und einfachen Formen basiert, sehr schick wirken. Die Lichtreflexe auf der Metallelementen und die helle Beleuchtung verleihen einer Umgebung Glanz, die vor allem Eleganz sucht.

Les réminiscences du style des années cinquante transmettent une touche très élégante à partir de formes droites et simples. Les reflets des éléments métalliques et l'éclairage abondant parachèvent la splendeur d'un espace qui cherche l'élégance pardessus de tout.

Las reminiscencias del estilo de los años cincuenta proporcionan un toque chic a base de formas rectas y simples. Los reflejos de los elementos metálicos y la profusa iluminación acaban de dar esplendor a un espacio que busca la elegancia por encima de todo.

Le reminiscenze dello stile degli anni cinquanta danno un tocco chic a base di forme rette e semplici. I riflessi degli elementi metallici e la profusa illuminazione finiscono col dare splendore ad uno spazio che cerca soprattutto eleganza.

42, avenue Montaigne, 75008 Paris, France Tel. +39 1 47 23 74 12
www.chanel.com

Chanel

Architect: Peter Marino & Asociates **Photographer:** © David Cardelús

Dark shelves and walls framing the fixtures display accessories, in such a way that despite the great variety of products, they are all ordered in a similar way. This leaves the central spaces free for minor decorative items.

Die dunklen Regale und Wände umrahmen die Lichtpunkte, in denen die Accessoires ausgestellt werden, so dass die Produkte trotz ihrer Verschiedenheit und Vielfältigkeit geordnet wirken. Außerdem kann man so die Mitte der Räume bis auf kleine dekorative Objekte frei lassen.

Les étagères et les murs sombres encadrent les points de lumière où sont exposés les accessoires, qui en dépit de leur diversité, sont tous rangés de la même manière. Le centre des espaces, ainsi libéré, est réservé aux petits détails.

Las estanterías y paredes oscuras enmarcan los puntos de luz donde se exhiben los complementos, de manera que, a pesar de la diversidad de productos, todos están ordenados de la misma manera. Así se consigue dejar el centro de los espacios libre, tan sólo ocupados por pequeños detalles.

Le scaffalature e le pareti scure incorniciano i punti luce dove sono esposti gli accessori, in modo tale che nonostante la diversità dei prodotti, tutti sono ordinati nello stesso modo. Si riesce così a lasciare il centro degli spazi liberi, occupati solo da piccoli dettagli.

54, avenue Montaigne, 75008 Paris, France Tel. +33 1 45 62 47 00

www.vuitton.com

Louis Vuitton

Architect: Peter Marino **Photographer:** © Roger Casas

Rich, sumptuous materials highlight the appeal and elegance of this interior, with its abundance of space to display the clothes. The grand staircase is a dramatic centrepiece that emphasises the brand's timeless stylishness.

Die edlen Materialien, die benutzt wurden, unterstreichen die wundervolle Gestaltung dieser einladenden und eleganten Räume, die viel Platz bieten, um die Kleidungsstücke auszustellen. Die beeindruckende Treppe im Inneren wirkt wie in Bühnenelement und unterstreicht die zeitlose Eleganz der Marke.

La richesse des matériaux utilisés rehausse la qualité du design d'un intérieur accueillant et élégant, disposant d'un espace suffisant pour exposer facilement les vêtements. Le grand escaliere met en scène l'intérieur tout en réaffirmant l'élégance intemporelle de la marque.

La riqueza de los materiales utilizados realza la calidad del diseño de un interior acogedor y elegante, donde hay suficiente espacio para exponer las prendas sin interferencias. La gran escalinata se transforma en un elemento escenográfico del interior y reafirma la elegancia atemporal de la marca.

La ricchezza dei materiali usati evidenzia la qualità del design di un interno accogliente ed elegante, in cui vi è spazio sufficiente per esporre, senza interferenze, i capi. La grande scalinata conferisce un elemento scenografico all'ambiente, raffermando, inoltre, l'eleganza senza tempo della marca.

15 Duke of York Square, London SW3 4LY, U.K. Tel. +44 20 7259 0777
www.tateossian.com

Tateossian London

Designer: Robert Tateossian **Photographer:** © Roger Casas

All the shop windows, within and without, are based on the same modular element, in such a way that although they are not all identical, they give order to the walls inside the shop. A large, circular table in the center serves as counterpoint to the cubes, besides being very useful to staff.

Alle Schaufenster, innen und außen, basieren auf dem gleichen Modul, so dass sie, obwohl sie nicht identisch sind, den Wänden des Shops eine Ordnung verleihen. Im Zentrum befindet sich ein großer, runder Ladentisch, der als Kontrapunkt zu diesen Modulen dient und außerdem für die Mitarbeiter nützlich ist.

Toutes les devantures, intérieures ou extérieures, se basent sur le même module, de sorte que sans être identiques elles parviennent à agencer tous les murs de la boutique. Au centre, un grand comptoir circulaire contraste avec les modules, tout en étant un outil très utile aux employés.

Todos los escaparates, ya sean interiores o exteriores, se basan en el mismo módulo, de manera que aunque no sean iguales consiguen ordenar todos los muros de la tienda. En el centro, un gran mostrador circular hace de contrapunto a los módulos, además de ser una herramienta muy útil para sus trabajadores.

Tutte le vetrine, interne od esterne, seguono lo stesso modulo, e pur non essendo uguali riescono ad ordinare tutti i muri del negozio. Al centro, un gran banco circolare fa da contrappunto ai moduli, oltre ad essere un elemento molto utile per i suoi dipendenti.

20 Via Montenapoleone, 20121 Milan, Italy Tel. +39 027 602 0285
www.valentino.it

Valentino

Architect: Antonio Citterio and Partners **Photographer:** © Gabriele Basilisco

This shop is designed as a series of rooms, which customers can use exclusively by themselves, as though they were at home in their dressing room. These semi-private rooms help to create a sense of uniqueness and quality around the product.

Dieser Shop ist wie eine Aufeinanderfolge von Zimmern angelegt, die zu exklusiven Räumen für die Kunden werden können, die sich so fühlen, als ob sie in ihrem eigenen Ankleidezimmer wären. Diese halb privaten Räume unterstreichen das außergewöhnliche Markenimage und die Qualität der Produkte.

La boutique est conçue comme un ensemble d'habitations, fonctionnant à l'instar de lieux exclusifs pour ses clients, afin qu'ils se sentent comme s'ils étaient dans leur propre dressing. Ces espaces semi privés exaltent le caractère exceptionnel de la marque et la qualité de ses produits.

La tienda está pensada como un conjunto de habitaciones que pueden funcionar como lugares exclusivos para los clientes, para que se sientan como si estuvieran en su propio vestidor. Con estos espacios semiprivados se remarca la excepcionalidad de la marca y la calidad de sus productos.

Il negozio è concepito come un complesso di stanze che possono fungere da luoghi esclusivi per i clienti, per permettere loro di sedersi come se si trovassero nel proprio spogliatoio. Con questi spazi semiprivati, si sottolinea l'eccezionalità della marca e la qualità dei suoi prodotti.

60, avenue Montaigne, 75008 Paris, France Tel. +33 1 56 69 80 80

www.gucci.com

Gucci

Architect: William Sofield **Photographer:** © Roger Casas

The spaciousness of the shop allows a very sophisticated decoration scheme, but without the structural aspects dominating the impact of the range of clothing. The large entrance stairway proclaims the lavishness of the interior, even though this is a feature from the original building.

Da dieses Lokal sehr groß ist, konnte man es sehr edel dekorieren, ohne dass die architektonischen Elemente der Markenkleidung, die hier verkauft wird, die Show stehlen. Die große Treppe am Eingang kündigt den Reichtum des Inneren bereits an, obwohl es sich um ein architektonisches Element des Originalgebäudes handelt.

L'amplitude de la boutique permet de déployer une décoration très sophistiquée, sans que les éléments architecturaux n'accaparent l'attention plus que les vêtements de marque. Le grand perron de l'entrée augure de la richesse intérieure, même si c'est un élément architectural de l'édifice original.

La amplitud de la tienda permite desarrollar una decoración muy sofisticada, sin que los elementos arquitectónicos acaparen el protagonismo ante la ropa de la marca. La gran escalinata de la entrada, un elemento arquitectónico del edificio original, anuncia la riqueza del interior.

La dimensione del negozio consente di sviluppare un arredamento molto raffinato, senza che gli elementi architettonici accaparrino il protagonismo a scapito dei capi della marca. La grande scalinata dell'ingresso annuncia la ricchezza dell'interno, pur trattandosi di un elemento architettonico dell'edificio originale.

14-16, rue du Faubourg Saint-Honoré, 75008 Paris, France Tel. +33 1 42 65 59 70
www.bottegaveneta.com

Bottega Veneta

Architect: Tomas Maier and William Sofield **Photographer:** © Roger Casas

The wooden slats at the rear of the display cabinet are an ingenious solution to permit light to enter whilst also creating a visual barrier between the interior and exterior. The warmth of the wood is repeated in other materials such as leather or carpet.

Die Holzlamellen bilden den Hintergrund der Schaufenster und sind gleichzeitig eine vorzügliche Lösung, um Licht durchzulassen und gleichzeitig eine visuelle Barriere zwischen innen und außen zu schaffen. Die Wärme des Holzes wird mit anderen Materialien, wie Leder und Teppichboden, wiederholt.

Les lames de bois qui composent le fond de la devanture, sont une solution ingénieuse pour laisser passer la lumière tout en créant une barrière visuelle entre l'extérieur et l'intérieur. La chaleur du bois se retrouve dans d'autres matériaux, comme le cuir ou la moquette.

Las lamas de madera que constituyen el fondo del escaparate son una ingeniosa solución para dejar pasar la luz y, al mismo tiempo, crear una barrera visual entre el exterior y el interior. La calidez de la madera se repite en otros materiales, como el cuero o la moqueta.

Le lame di legno che costituiscono il fondo della vetrina, sono un'ingegnosa soluzione per lasciar passare la luce e, allo stesso tempo, creare una barriera visiva tra l'esterno e l'interno. Il calore del legno si ritrova in altri materiali, come il cuoio o la moquette.

Trash-Chic

Laundry Industry

Desigual

Junky Styling

Camper

Dover Street Market

Vivienne Westwood

10500 Hairdressers

186 Westbourne Grove, London W11 2RH, U.K. Tel. +44 20 7792 7967
www.laundryindustry.com

Laundry Industry

Designer: Laundry Industry **Photographer:** © Roger Casas

Different levels inside the shop produce a descending gradient that is not apparent from the outside. The doors, service counters, cash desks and clothes racks are all perpendicular to the customer, which draws attention to the singularity of the floor space.

Der Höhenunterschied im Inneren macht aus dem Boden des Shops eine Rampe nach unten, deren Neigung man von außen nicht wahrnehmen kann. Die Türen, die Kassentheke und die Kleiderständer stehen wie die Menschen im Lot, was den einzigartigen Boden noch betont.

La dénivellation intérieure transforme le sol de la boutique en pente douce, inclinaison invisible de l'extérieur. Les portes, le comptoir de la caisse et les portemanteaux sont perpendiculaires à la verticalité humaine, ce qui accentue l'originalité du sol.

El desnivel del interior convierte el suelo de la tienda en una rampa descendente, a pesar de que su inclinación no se percibe desde el exterior. Las puertas, el mostrador de la caja y los percheros son perpendiculares a la verticalidad humana, lo que acentúa la singularidad del suelo.

Il dislivello dell'interno trasforma il pavimento del negozio in una rampa discendente, sebbene la sua inclinazione non si percepisce dall'esterno. Le porte, il banco della cassa e gli appendiabiti sono perpendicolari alla verticale umana, cosa che accentua la singolarità del pavimento.

Argenteria 65, 08003 Barcelona, Spain Tel. +34 933 103 015
www.desigual.com

Desigual

Designer: Martí Guixé Photographer: © Imagekontainer

This shop displays clothes in a very unconventional manner; taped to the wall or scattered around the entrance, as if the show window had spread and invaded the hallway. This casual mise-en-scène contrasts sharply with the orderly interior, where each garment is in its place.

Die Kleidung wird in diesem Shop auf eine ungezwungene Art ausgestellt. So wird sie zum Beispiel mit einem Band an der Wand befestigt oder sie liegt ungeordnet am Eingang herum, so als ob sich das Schaufenster über die gesamte Eingangshalle des Lokals ausgebreitet hätte. Diese wie zufällig wirkende Inszenierung steht im Gegensatz zu der Ordnung, die im Inneren herrscht, wo jedes Kleidungsstück an seinem Platz ist.

Dans cette boutique la manière d'exposer les vêtements est décontractée : ils sont suspendus sur un cintre accroché au mur ou éparpillés en désordre à l'entrée, comme si la devanture s'était étendue dans de tout le hall de la boutique. Cette scénographie « désinvolte » contraste avec l'ordre qui règne à l'intérieur, où chaque vêtement à sa place attitrée.

En esta tienda la manera de exponer la ropa es desenfadada; se engancha con cinta a la pared o se distribuye desordenadamente por la entrada, como si el escaparate se hubiera expandido por todo el hall de la tienda. Esta escenografía "casual" contrasta con el orden que reina en el interior, donde cada prenda tiene su lugar.

In questo negozio i capi sono esposti in modo informale; si agganciano con dello scotch alla parete o si distribuiscono in modo disordinato all'ingresso, come se la vetrina si fosse estesa al hall del negozio. Questa scenografia "casual" contrasta con l'ordine che regna dentro, ove ogni capo ha un suo posto.

12 Dray Walk, The Old Brewery, 91 Brick Lane, London E2 6RF, U.K. Tel. +44 20 7247 1883
www.junkystyling.co.uk

Junky Styling

Designers: Annika Sanders, Kerry Seager **Photographer:** © Roger Casas

The balance between old furniture and new wrought iron fixtures follows the same guiding principle as when old-fashioned clothes are re-tailored to new styles. The feature details of the garment design are transposed into the mise-en-scène so that an unaffected effect is produced throughout.

Die Mischung aus alten Möbeln und neuen Elementen aus Schmiedeeisen entspricht dem Stil der Kleidermarke, die aus der Mode gekommene Kleidung benutzt, um sie mit neuen Schnitten umzunähen. Der Blick fürs Detail beim Entwurf der Kleider findet ihren Niederschlag einer sorgfältigen Präsentation. Die Umgebung wirkt ungezwungen, ebenso wie die ausgestellte Kleidung.

Le mélange entre meubles anciens et éléments nouveaux en fer forgé est à l'image du style développé par la marque de confection qui réutilise des habits démodés pour en faire de nouveaux modèles. L'amour du détail dans la conception de cette ligne vestimentaire se traduit par une mise en scène parfaitement étudiée où règne une ambiance décontractée, à l'instar des vêtements exposés.

La mezcla entre los muebles antiguos y los nuevos elementos de hierro forjado sigue el mismo estilo que la marca de ropa, que reutiliza trajes pasados de moda para recoserlos con nuevos patrones. El detallismo del diseño de la ropa se traduce en una cuidada puesta en escena, donde reina un ambiente desenfadado, como la ropa expuesta.

Il mélange tra i mobili antichi ed i nuovi elementi di ferro battuto è in linea con lo stile della marca d'abbigliamento, che riutilizza i vestiti passati di moda ricucendoli con nuovi modelli. L'attenzione del dettaglio del design dei capi d'abbigliamento si traduce in una curata messa in scena dove regna un ambiente rilassato, come i capi esposti.

Pelayo 13–37, 08001 Barcelona, Spain Tel. +34 933 024 124

www.camper.com

Camper

Designers: Martí Guixé and estudio Camper **Photographer:** © Alejandro Bachrach

The simple, effective design uses Velcro strips to suspend shoes, thus displaying the product without showcases. The urban, casual style is backed by the plainness of the surrounding decor, clearly exaggerated by the understated staircase on the main wall inside the shop.

Einfachheit und Effektivität sind die Grundlage dieses Designs. Die Schuhe sind an Klettbändern befestigt, so sind keine Ausstellungselemente für die Produkte notwendig. Der urbane und lockere Stil wird durch die einfache Dekoration unterstrichen, die die gezackte Linie der Treppe an der Hauptwand des Shops in die Gestaltung einbezieht.

La simplicité et l'efficacité sont la base de ce design qui utilise des bandes de velcro pour accrocher les chaussures afin d'exposer le produit sans présentoir. Le style urbain et casuel est exalté par la simplicité de la décoration, qui accentue délibérément la ligne coupée de l'escalier sur le mur principal de la boutique.

La simpleza y efectividad es la base de este diseño, que recurre a cintas de velcro en las que se enganchan los zapatos para mostrar el producto sin necesidad de expositores. El estilo urbano y casual queda reforzado por la simpleza de la decoración, que acentúa sin prejuicios la línea recortada de la escalera en el muro principal de la tienda.

La semplicità e l'effettività è la base di questo design, che ricorre a strisce di velcro sui cui sono agganciate le scarpe per mostrare il prodotto senza dover ricorrere agli espositori. Lo stile urbano e casual è rafforzato dalla semplicità dell'arredamento, che accentua senza pregiudizio la linea della scala ritagliata sul muro principale del negozio.

17–18 Dover Street, London W1S 4NL, U.K. Tel. +44 20 7518 0680

Dover Street Market

Architect: Rei Kawakubo Photographer: © Roger Casas

This fashion market is located in an old London industrial building, whose restructuring entailed removing partition walls to open up as much space as possible. Although it may appear to be perpetually under construction, it is in fact a very versatile locale where the décor is readily customizable for every circumstance.

Dieser Trendmarkt befindet sich in einem alten Industriegebäude in London, bei dessen Umbau Trennwände niedergerissen und der Raum so weit wie möglich geöffnet wurde. Es scheint zwar so, als werde der Raum ständig umgebaut, doch in Wirklichkeit ist er veränderbar und kann für jede neue Präsentation wieder anders gestaltet werden.

Un vieil édifice industriel londonien abrite ce marché de boutiques tendance, dont la rénovation a permis d'ôter les cloisons pour ouvrir l'espace le plus possible. Même avec ses allures de chantier éternel, il s'agit d'un espace facilement modulable, dont les finitions se modifient au gré des nouvelles mises en scènes.

En un viejo edificio industrial londinense encontramos este mercado de tendencias, cuya remodelación consistió en tirar tabiques y abrir el espacio en la medida de lo posible. Aunque parezca estar permanentemente en obras, se trata de un espacio fácilmente modificable, y los acabados se deciden con cada nueva puesta en escena.

Questo mercato di tendenze si trova in un vecchio edificio industriale londinese dove sono stati buttati giù i tramezzi, ed aperto lo spazio per quanto possibile. Pur sembrando che i lavori sono perennemente in corso, è uno spazio facilmente modificabile, e le rifiniture sono decise ogni volta che si sceglie la messa in scena.

44 Conduit Street, London W1S 2YL, U.K. Tel. +44 20 7439 1109
www.viviennewestwood.com

Vivienne Westwood

Designer: Vivienne Westwood **Photographer:** © Roger Casas

The paradoxical world of Vivienne Westwood, a blend of sumptuous, urban, aristocratic and lower-class elements, is reflected by the coexistence of wood bark, old display cases and 19th century furniture.

Das paradoxe Universum von Vivienne Westwood, das irgendwo zwischen luxuriös und urban, aristokratisch und "lower-class" liegt, spiegelt sich in diesem Shop wider, in dem Baumrinden mit alten Ladentischen und Möbeln aus dem 19. Jahrhundert kombiniert werden.

L'univers paradoxal de Vivienne Westwood, entre somptueux et urbain, entre aristocratie et "lower-class", se reflète dans cette boutique où se côtoient écorces d'arbres, comptoirs anciens et meubles du XIXe siècle.

El paradójico universo de Vivienne Westwood, entre suntuoso y urbano, entre aristócrata y "lower-class", queda reflejado en esta tienda donde conviven cortezas de árboles con mostradores antiguos y muebles del siglo XIX.

Il paradossale universo di Vivienne Westwood, tra il sontuoso e l'urbano, tra l'aristocratico e il "lower-class", si riflette in questo negozio ove convivono cortecce d'alberi con banchi antichi e mobili del XIX secolo.

284 Westbourne Park Road, London W11 1EH, U.K. Tel. +44 20 7229 3777
www.10500hair.com

10500 Hairdressers

Architect: Andy Martins Associates **Photographer:** © Roger Casas

In order to transform this space, which includes a basement, into a designer hairdressing salon, the maximum possible amount of light was allowed to stream into the interior. To this end a glass show-case occupied the front of the salon and an open spiral staircase permitted light to enter the lower floor.

Um diese Räume, zu denen ein Kellergeschoss gehört, in einen modernen Friseursalon umzugestalten, versuchte man, soviel Licht wie möglich ins Innere zu leiten. Dazu schuf man ein Schaufenster, das die gesamte Fassade einnimmt und eine Wendeltreppe, die so weit offen wie möglich ist, damit das Licht auch in das untere Stockwerk fällt.

Pour transformer cet espace doté d'un sous-sol en un salon de coiffure design, l'accent a été mis sur l'optimalisation de la lumière extérieure vers l'intérieur en créant une devanture de verre qui occupe la façade et un escalier en colimaçon le plus ouvert possible, qui laisse passer la lumière vers l'étage inférieur.

Para transformar este espacio con sótano en una peluquería de diseño se recurrió a proporcionar el máximo de luz posible al interior mediante un escaparate de cristal que ocupa la fachada y una escalera de caracol lo más abierta posible, que deja pasar la luz al piso inferior.

Per trasformare questo spazio con piano interrato in un parrucchiere di design si è scelto di dare la massima luce possibile agli interni mediante una vetrina di cristallo che occupa la facciata ed una scala a chiocciola, il più aperta possibile, che lascia passare la luce al piano inferiore.

Mise-en-scène

136, avenue des Champs-Elysées, 75008 Paris, France Tel. +33 1 42 89 30 20
www.peugeot.com

Peugeot Avenue

Architect: Saguez & Partners and Versions **Photographer:** © Roger Casas

The Peugeot showroom is redecorated every three months; the interior space is reinvented each time with a new design. This was the case with the "circus" theme which was currently on view when the photographic report was carried out. With such a well thought-out mise-en-scène, Peugeot Avenue becomes a recreational space rather than just a shop.

Im Showroom von Peugeot wird die Dekoration alle drei Monate verändert und der Raum nach neuen Themen gestaltet. Als diese Fotoreportage entstand, lautete das Leitmotiv zum Beispiel Zirkus. Dank sorgfältigen Inszenierung wird Peugeot Avenue zu einem Ort der Freizeitgestaltung und weniger zu einem Verkaufsraum.

Le « showroom » Peugeot renouvelle sa décoration tous les trois mois, réinventant l'espace sur des thèmes nouveaux, à l'instar du cirque, qui en était le « leitmotiv » au moment du reportage photographique. Grâce à cette mise en scène étudiée, Peugeot Avenue se convertit en espace ludique plus qu'en magasin.

El "showroom" Peugeot renueva la decoración cada tres meses, de manera que cada vez el espacio se reinventa con temas nuevos, como el circo, que era el "leitmotiv" en el momento en que se hizo el reportaje fotográfico. Con esta cuidada puesta en escena, Peugeot Avenue se convierte en un espacio lúdico más que en una tienda al uso.

Lo "showroom" Peugeot rinnova l'arredamento ogni tre mesi, in modo che ogni volta lo spazio è reinventato con nuovi temi, come il circo, che era il "leit motif" nel momento in cui è stato fatto il servizio fotografico. Con questa curata messa in scena, Peugeot Avenue diventa più uno spazio ludico che in un negozio al consumo.

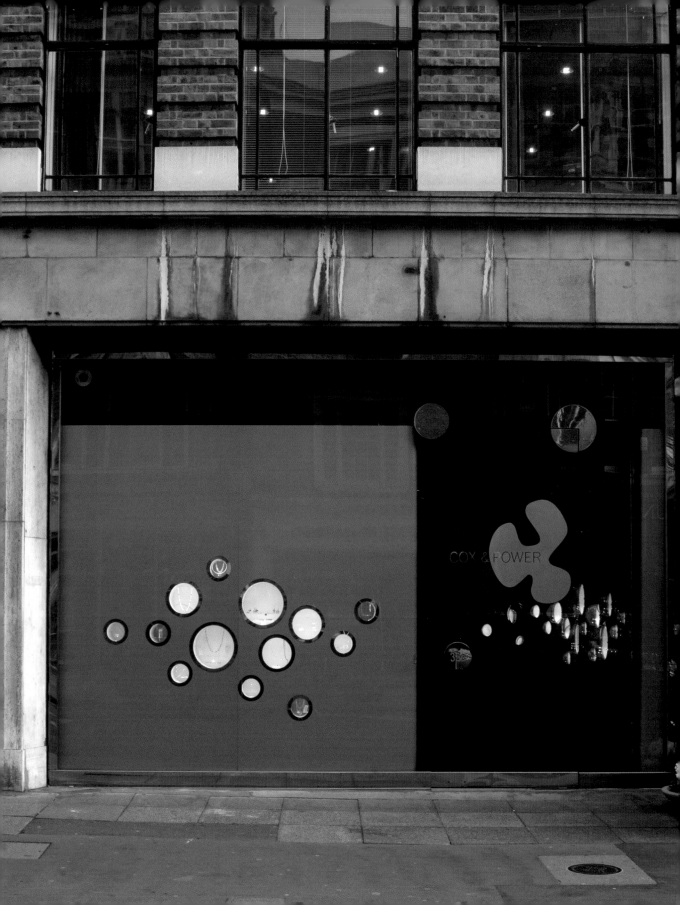

35c Marylebone High Street, London W1U 4QA, U.K. Tel. +44 20 7935 3530
www.coxandpower.com

Cox & Power

Architect: Sybarite Photographer: © Roger Casas

Blown glass ornaments serve as displays for jewellery, and also add character to an otherwise austere and serene interior. Once again, Sybarite achieves the perfect design solution for the specific needs of the shop: to showcase jewels in a simple and eye-catching manner at the same time creating a unique and appealing setting .

Objekte aus geblasenen Glas dienen als Ausstellungselemente für Schmuck und sind eine besondere Attraktion in dem sonst schlichten und heiteren Ambiente. Sybarite hat wieder einmal die perfekte Lösung für diesen speziellen Kunden gefunden: Der Schmuck wird auf einfache und angenehme Weise ausgestellt, zugleich wird eine einzigartige Umgebung geschaffen, die den Blick fesselt.

Les pièces en verre soufflé qui servent de supports à ces bijoux, sont la grande attraction de cet intérieur austère et serein. Une fois de plus, Sybarite parvient à concevoir une solution parfaitement adaptée aux besoins spécifiques de la boutique : exposer les bijoux de manière agréable et simple tout en créant un espace unique qui attire le regard.

Las piezas de vidrio soplado sirven de expositor para estas joyas, y son la gran atracción de este interior austero y sereno. Una vez más, Sybarite consigue diseñar la solución perfecta para las necesidades específicas de la tienda: mostrar las joyas de forma sencilla y agradable y al mismo tiempo crear un espacio único y llamativo.

I pezzi di vetro soffiato servono da espositore per questi gioielli, e sono la grand'attrazione di questi interni austeri e sereni. Ancora una volta, Sibarite riesce a concepire la perfetta soluzione per le specifiche necessità del negozio: mostrare i gioielli in modo semplice e gradevole ed, allo stesso tempo, creare uno spazio unico che salta agli occhi.

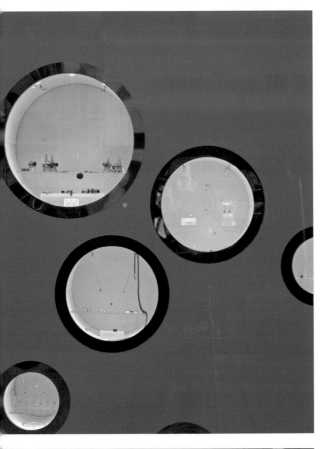
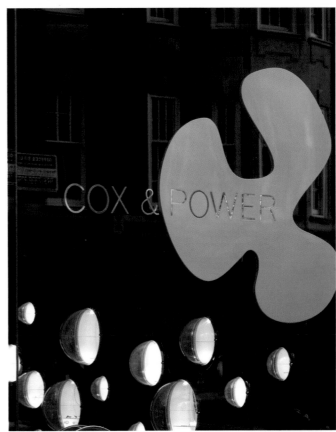

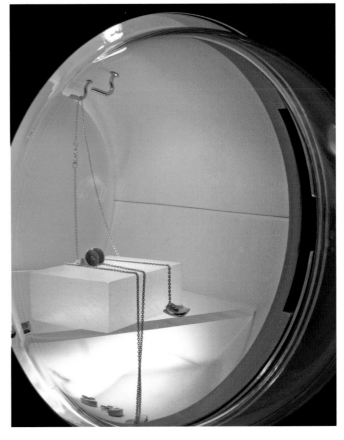

150 New Bond Street, London W1S 2TT, U.K. Tel. +44 20 7629 0550
www.emanuelungaro.com

Emanuel Ungaro

Architect: Antonio Citterio **Photographer:** © Roger Casas

The combination of domestic elements with tinted glass and large well lit areas gives the customer the feeling of being at home, but without losing the commercial purpose of the space. The layout into different zones, as though entering different stalls, adds special congeniality to the premises.

Die Kombination von häuslichen Elementen mit gefärbtem Glas und hell erleuchteten Bereichen schafft eine Umgebung, in der sich der Kunde wie zuhause fühlt, ohne dass der Shop seine Verkaufsfunktion einbüßt. Die verschiedenen Bereiche sind so aufgeteilt, als ob es sich um verschiedene Zimmer handelte. Das macht diesen Shop warm und einladend.

Le mélange d'objets domestiques à des verres teintés et à de grands faisceaux de lumière fait que le client se sente comme chez lui, sans que l'espace perde pour autant sa fonction commerciale. L'organisation en zones, à l'instar de différents espaces de vie, rend cette boutique particulièrement chaleureuse.

La combinación de elementos domésticos con cristales tintados y grandes haces de luz hace posible que el cliente se sienta como en casa, pero sin que el espacio pierda su función comercial. La distribución por zonas, como si se tratara de distintas estancias, proporciona a esta tienda una calidez especial.

L'abbinamento d'elementi domestici con vetri tinti e grandi fasci di luce consente al cliente di sentirsi come a casa, ma senza far perdere la funzione commerciale allo spazio. La distribuzione per zone, come se si trattasse di varie sale, conferisce a questo negozio un calore speciale.

38 Dover Street, London W1S 4NL, U.K. Tel. +44 20 7408 0320

www.erco.com

Erco

Architect: Ken Shuttleworth / MAKE **Photographer:** © Roger Casas

The major protagonist in this shopping space is the lighting, which is continually changing. The different areas are decorated with very few objects—a picture, a vase, a pedestal—allowing customers to appreciate the full effect of the lighting.

Der absolute Hauptdarsteller in diesen Räumer ist das Licht, das sich ständig verändert. Die verschiedenen Bereiche sind mit sehr wenigen Objekten dekoriert – einem Bild, einem Krug und einem Sockel–und wenn man diese Objekte betrachtet, erkennt man alle Möglichkeiten der Beleuchtung.

La lumière qui est le protagoniste sans conteste de cette boutique, change constamment. Les divers espaces sont décorés avec parcimonie – un cadre, une cruche, un socle – ce qui permet au client d'apprécier la variété des éclairages.

La protagonista absoluta de esta tienda es la luz, que va cambiando constantemente a lo largo del día. Los diferentes espacios se decoran con muy pocos objetos –un cuadro, un jarrón, una peana–, y al observarlos el cliente puede apreciar todas sus posibilidades de iluminación.

La protagonista assoluta di questo negozio è la luce, che varia costantemente. I vari spazi sono arredati con pochissimi oggetti – un quadro, un vaso, una pedana –, e osservandoli, il cliente può apprezzare tutte le sue possibilità d'illuminazione.

53, avenue Montaigne, 75008 Paris, France Tel. +33 1 56 88 12 12
www.calvinklein.com

Calvin Klein

Architect: John Pawson **Photographer:** © Vincent Knapp

sortie de
secours

The sobriety and quality of this shop space reflect the idea of modern luxury sought by this brand. The constant features are light colors and flawless lighting, avoiding any strident note. The models are in unusual poses, as though living and having a conversation among themselves.

Die schlichte und hochwertige Gestaltung dieses Raumes spiegelt die Idee von modernem Luxus wider, den diese Marke anstrebt. Die hellen Farben und die perfekte Beleuchtung, die niemals grell ist, sind Konstanten, die sich durch den gesamten Raum ziehen. Die Schaufensterpuppen nehmen seltsame Positionen ein, so als ob sie lebendig wären und miteinander reden würden.

Le design de l'espace, sobre et de grande qualité, reflète l'idée de luxe moderne recherchée par la marque. Les couleurs claires et la perfection de l'éclairage sont une constante qui marque l'espace, évitant ainsi les fausses notes. Les mannequins sont disposés dans des poses étranges, comme s'ils étaient vivants et parlaient entre eux.

El diseño sobrio y de gran calidad del espacio refleja la idea de lujo moderno que busca la marca. La constante de todo el espacio son los colores claros y la perfecta iluminación, con lo cual se evitan las estridencias. Los maniquíes están dispuestos en extrañas poses, como si estuvieran vivos y hablaran entre sí.

Il disegno sobrio e d'alta qualità dello spazio riflette l'idea di lusso moderno voluto dalla marca. La costante di tutto lo spazio sono i colori chiari e la perfetta illuminazione, che consente di evitare effetti stridenti. I manichini disposti in atteggiamenti strani, sembrano vivi e paiono conversare tra loro.

30 Bruton Street, London W1J 6LG, U.K. Tel. +44 20 7518 3100
www.stellamccartney.com

Stella McCartney

Designer: Stella McCartney **Photographer:** © Roger Casas

The large pink display cabinet in the center of the shop allows movement around both sides without assigning any area exclusively to sales assistants. In this way the customer may move freely around the entire space, which is open plan, as seen in particular at the rear of the premises where the boundary with the courtyard consists entirely of glass walls and ceiling, without a metal framework.

Der große rosafarbene Ladentisch mitten im Shop lässt den Durchgang auf beiden Seiten zu, ohne dass es einen Platz gibt, der ausschließlich dem Verkäufer vorbehalten ist. So kann der Kunde sich in den offenen Raümen frei bewegen, bis hin zum hinteren Teil, wo ein Innenhof mit einer Glaswand abgeschlossen und mit einem Glasdach überdeckt wurde, das nicht einmal Metallprofile besitzt.

Le grand comptoir rose situé au centre de la boutique laisse le passage libre des deux côtés, sans emplacement réservé au vendeur. De cette façon le client peut circuler partout, dans cet espace très ouvert, comme le démontre la partie arrière, dotée d'un patio recouvert d'une toiture et de parois tout en verre, sans aucun profil métallique.

El gran mostrador rosa situado en medio de la tienda permite el paso por ambos lados, sin que haya un lugar especialmente reservado para el dependiente. De esta manera el cliente puede circular por todo el espacio, como lo demuestra la parte posterior, donde el cerramiento sobre el patio está formado por muros y techo de cristal sin ningún perfil metálico.

Il gran bancone situato in mezzo al negozio consente il passaggio sui due lati, senza esserci un posto riservato per il dipendente. In tal modo, il cliente può circolare in tutto lo spazio, che è molto aperto, come lo dimostra la parte posteriore, in cui la chiusura sul cortile è realizzata con muri e tetti di vetro, privi del minimo profilato metallico.

43 Greene Street, New York, NY 10013, USA Tel. +1 212 334 7130
www.bisazza.com

Bisazza Mosaico
Showroom & Gallery

Architect: Fabio Novembre **Photographer:** © Alberto Ferrero

The showroom is designed as an interior landscape to display all aspects of the mosaics, in such a way that the display is the shop itself rather than product samples. The centerpiece, which serves as a settee, is reminiscent of a medusa, which is in line with the other marine features in the composition.

Um alle Eigenschaften des Mosaiks zu zeigen, ist der Showroom wie eine innere Landschaft angelegt, so dass man das Geschäftslokal und nicht die Ausstellung eines Produktes betrachtet. Das Teil in der Mitte, das als Sofa dienen kann, erinnert an eine Medusa inmitten der Anspielungen auf das Wasser, die es in diesem Raum gibt.

Pour exalter toutes les qualités de la mosaïque, le « showroom » est conçu comme un paysage intérieur, de sorte que l'on contemple la boutique en elle-même et non l'échantillon du produit. L'élément central qui peut servir de sofa, rappelle une méduse au cœur des réminiscences aquatiques de la boutique.

Para mostrar todas las cualidades del mosaico, el "showroom" se concibe como un paisaje interior, de manera que lo que se contempla es la tienda en sí y no el muestrario del producto. La pieza del medio, que puede servir de sofá, recuerda a una medusa en medio de las reminiscencias acuáticas de la tienda.

Per mostrare tutte le qualità del mosaico, lo "showroom" è concepito come un paesaggio interno, in modo che quello che si vede è il negozio e non il campionario del prodotto. Il pezzo centrale, che può servire anche da divano, ricorda una medusa nel bel mezzo delle reminiscenze acquatiche del negozio.

Urban

Energie

Mathmos

Clear

Hare

Knoll International

Poliform

Pilma

Greek

Kode

La Ciénaga

I.a. Eyeworks

Face à Face

47-49 Neal Street, London, WC2H 9P2, U.K. Tel. +44 20 7836 7719
www.energie.it

Energie

Architect: Studio 63 associati **Photographer:** © Yael Pincus

This brand's urban style is displayed in a setting reminiscent of the nineteen-fifties, in such a way that the contrasts highlight the product's modern qualities and capacity for integration with other cult objects.

Der urbane Stil der Marke wird in einer Umgebung im Retrostil der Fünfzigerjahre ausgestellt, so dass dieser Gegensatz die Modernität der Marke und ihre Fähigkeit zur Integration in eine Umgebung voller Designobjekte mit Kultcharakter noch unterstreicht.

Le style urbain de la marque est exposé dans une atmosphère rétro des années cinquante, contraste qui valorise la modernité de la marque et sa faculté d'intégrer des objets de design cultes.

El estilo urbano de la marca se expone en una ambientación retro de los años cincuenta, de manera que el contraste realza la modernidad de la marca y su capacidad de integración con objetos de diseño de culto.

Il giallo abbinato a questa marca è presente in tutto il negozio, dai fondi degli espositori al gran mobile in vinile che ricopre tutta la parete di fondo, o il bancone del mobile espositore centrale. Le pieghe degli scaffali servono ad esporre gli accessori e, allo stesso tempo, conferiscono dinamismo agli interni.

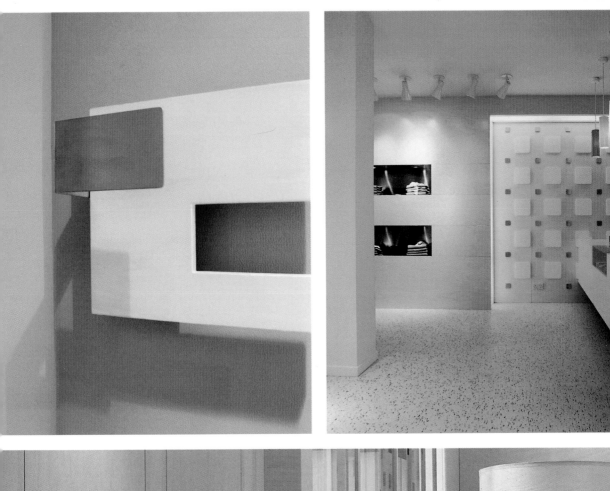

22-24 Old Street, London EC1V 9AP, U.K. Tel. +44 20 7549 2700

www.mathmos.com

Mathmos

Architects: Sam Hecht and Kim Collin / Industrial Facility **Photographer:** © Roger Casas

The renowned designs of Mathmos fixtures, with their rounded forms, are the central factor of this store. The facade is a seamless glass surface allowing full view of the shelves featuring cylindrical displays containing the lamps.

Die berühmten Designerlampen von Mathmos mit ihren runden Formen bilden zweifelsohne den Referenzpunkt in diesem Lokal. Die Fassade besteht aus einer Glaswand, durch die man die Regale mit den zylinderförmigen Ausstellungselementen für die Lampen sehen kann.

Les célèbres designs de lampe de Mathmos, aux formes arrondies, sont le symbole indiscutable de la boutique. La façade est constituée d'une enveloppe de verre teinté qui permet de voir les étagères avec des présentoirs cylindriques où les lampes sont exposées.

Los famosos diseños de lámparas de Mathmos, con sus formas redondeadas, son el referente indiscutible de la tienda. La fachada está formada por un cerramiento de cristal corrido que permite ver la estantería con muestrarios cilíndricos donde se exhiben las lámparas.

I famosi disegni delle lampade di Mathmos, con le loro forme arrotondate, sono il referente indiscutibile del negozio. La facciata è composta da un infisso di vetro continuo che consente di vedere la scaffalatura con i campionari cilindrici dove sono esposte le lampade.

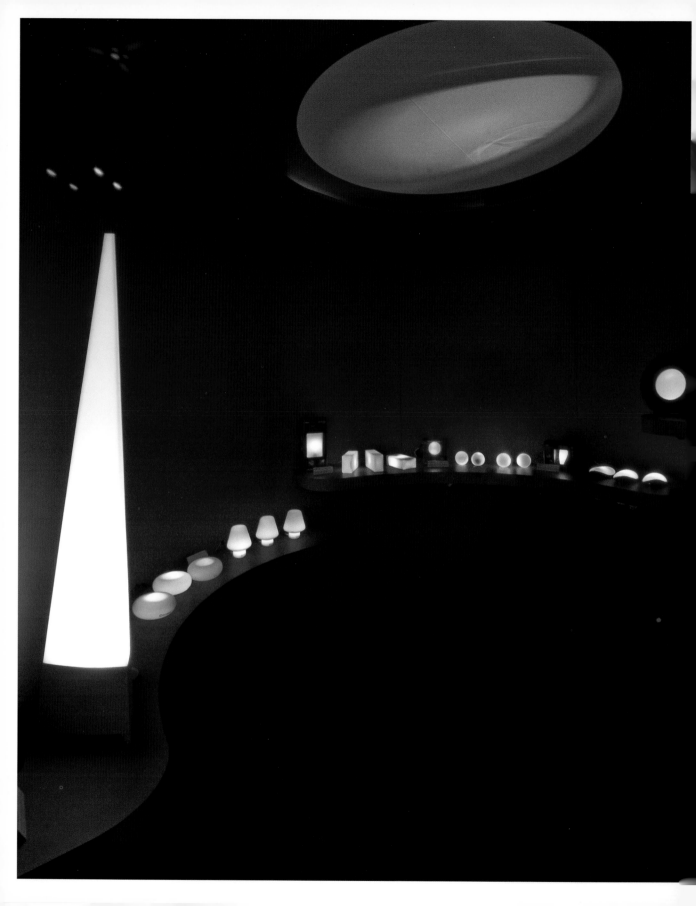

GRITO   **£55** Design: El Ultimo Grito

A spun aluminium lamp shade which simply slips over the light fitting without
the need to adapt the lead or remove the bulb. Available in neutral, blue
or red.

Pi 11 pral. 10, 08002 Barcelona, Spain Tel. +34 933 170 822

Clear

Architects: Yaya Tour, Coloco **Photographer:** © Alejandro Bachrach

Futuristic seating is the outstanding feature in this shop interior, which focuses the attention on the customer. The remainder of the decoration is anchored on this key element.

Die futuristischen Sitze sind das auffälligste Element dieses Shops, was dazu führt, dass sich die Aufmerksamkeit auf den Umgang mit dem Kunden konzentriert. Die übrige Dekoration des Shops bezieht sich auf dieses Element.

Les fauteuils futuristes sont l'élément le plus caractéristique de la boutique, de sorte que l'attention est centrée sur le client. Le reste de la décoration de la boutique tourne autour de cet élément.

Las butacas futuristas son el elemento más característico de la tienda, de manera que la atención se centra en el trato con el cliente. El resto de la decoración de la tienda gira alrededor de este elemento.

Le poltrone futuriste sono l'elemento più caratteristico del negozio, in modo tale che l'attenzione si centra sulla cura del cliente.

4-12-4 Minami Senba, Chuo-ku, Osaka, Japan Tel. +81 06 6110 7566

Hare

Architect: Tsutomu Kurokawa Photographer: © Kozo Takayama

An open gap connecting the two floors leaves wooden rafters in full view, involving the structure of the building in the shop interior decor. The fixtures hanging from the ceiling emulate drops of water and their apparent fragility underlines the central character of this space.

Die Öffnung zwischen dem ersten und dem zweiten Stock lässt die Holzbalken frei, so dass die Struktur des Gebäudes zu einem Teil der Dekoration des Shops wird. Die Lampen, die an der Decke hängen, gleichen Wassertropfen und unterstreichen mit ihrer Zerbrechlichkeit den Mittelpunkt des Lokals.

L'ouverture entre le premier et le deuxième étage permet de voir les poutres en bois, permettant d'intégrer la structure de l'édifice à la décoration de la boutique. Les lampes tombent du plafond à l'instar de gouttes d'eau soulignant la subtilité du centre de cet espace.

La abertura entre el primer y el segundo piso deja a la vista las vigas de madera, de manera que la estructura del edificio se incorpora a la decoración de la tienda. Las lámparas que cuelgan del techo parecen gotas de agua y acentúan con su fragilidad el carácter central de este espacio.

L'apertura tra il primo ed il secondo piano lascia alla vista le travi di legno, in modo tale che la struttura dell'edificio diventa parte dell'arredamento del negozio. Le lampade appese al tetto sembrano delle gocce d'acqua che accentuano con la loro fragilità la centralità di questo spazio.

268, boulevard Saint-Germain, 75007 Paris, France Tel. +33 1 44 18 19 99
www.knoll.com

Knoll International

Designer: Knoll Photographer: © Roger Casas

The wall mirrors and glass facade allow the space to remain undefined. The display strategy keeps the walls free by concentrating all the furniture in the central area.

Die Spiegel an den Wänden und das große Fenster an der Fassade lassen den Raum so offen wirken, dass der Blick nicht auf ein bestimmtes Ziel gerichtet ist. Die Strategie, die bei der Ausstellung der Möbel eingeschlagen wird, ist es, die Wände nackt zu lassen und alle Möbel im Zentrum des Verkaufs-raumes zu zeigen.

Les miroirs aux murs et la grande paroi de verre de la façade créent un espace sans objectif défini. La stratégie d'exposition des meubles est de laisser les murs dépouillés, en ramenant tous les meubles au centre de l'espace.

Los espejos de las paredes y la gran cristalera de la fachada consiguen que el espacio no tenga un obje-tivo definido. La estrategia para exponer los muebles es dejar las paredes desnudas, concentrando todos los muebles en el centro del espacio.

Gli specchi delle pareti e la gran vetrata della facciata fanno sì che lo spazio non abbia un obiettivo definito. La strategia per esporre i mobili è di lasciare le pareti nude, concentrando tutti i mobili nel centro dello spazio.

Wavy lines and organic shapes are this outlet's leitmotiv, and it is taken to the extreme by having the glass counter shaped in a curve to match the rest of the furniture. The only features with a square pattern are the floor tiles and parquet, and a degree of tension and movement are achieved by this contrasting effect.

Die geschwungenen Linien und organische Formen sind das Leitmotiv dieses Shops, das durchgängig eingesetzt wurde, so dass sogar das Glas an den Ausstellungselementen wie die übrigen Möbel gebogen ist. Die einzigen Elemente, die einem Raster folgen, sind die Böden mit Fliesen und Parkett. Dieser Gegensatz lässt eine gewisse Spannung entstehen und verleiht dem Shop mehr Leben.

Les lignes ondulées et les formes organiques sont le leitmotiv de la boutique, avec les verres des comptoirs qui se courbent comme le reste du mobilier. Les uniques éléments qui suivent un schéma réticulaire sont les sols dallés et les parquets, un contraste qui crée une tension et imprime un certain dynamisme à la boutique.

Las líneas onduladas y las formas orgánicas son el leitmotiv de la tienda, hasta el punto de que los cristales de los mostradores se curvan como el resto del mobiliario. Los únicos elementos que siguen un esquema reticular son los suelos de baldosas y de parquet, un contraste que crea tensión y otorga viveza a la tienda.

Le linee ondulate e le forme organiche sono il leitmotiv del negozio, sino al punto che i vetri dei banchi del negozio si curvano come il resto dei mobili. Gli unici elementi che seguono lo schema reticolare sono i pavimenti di mattonelle e di parquet, un contrasto che crea tensione e da vita al negozio.

2-4-1 Marunochi, Chiyoda-ku, Tokyo, Japan Tel. +81 03 5220 7568

Pinceau

Architect: Tsutomu Kurokawa Photographer: © Kozo Takayama

This mixture of materials and textures brings out the shop's distinct personality, and they coexist in perfect harmony despite their disparity thanks to exquisite design techniques. The shop space combines wood and mosaics, concrete and metal showcases and white shelves against open brick walls.

Der Charakter dieses Geschäftes zeigt sich in der Mischung von Materialien und Texturen, die aufgrund ihres gepflegten Designs trotz ihrer Verschiedenheit perfekt zusammenpassen. So wird in diesem Shop Holz mit Mosaiken kombiniert, unverputzter Beton mit den Ausstellungselementen aus Metall und Glas, und Wände aus unverputztem Ziegelstein mit weißen Regalen.

La personnalité de la boutique ressort dans le mélange de matériaux et de textures, qui malgré leur disparité, se marient parfaitement bien grâce à un design à caractère très urbain. La boutique offre donc un mélange de bois et de mosaïque, de béton brut avec des présentoirs de métal et de verre ou encore des murs en brique apparente dotés d'étagères blanches.

La personalidad de la tienda queda patente en la mezcla de materiales y texturas, que pese a su disparidad conviven perfectamente gracias a un cuidadísimo diseño. Así, en la tienda se mezcla madera con mosaico, hormigón crudo con expositores de metal y cristal o paredes de ladillo visto con estantes blancos.

La personalità del negozio è patente nell'abbinamento di materiali e tessiture, che nonostante la loro disparità convivono perfettamente grazie ad un design molto curato. Così, nel negozio si mischia legno con mosaico, cemento crudo con espositori in metallo o vetro, o pareti di mattoni a vista con ripiani bianchi.

3-11-7 Ichiban-cho, Aoba-ku, Sendai-Shi, Japan Tel. +81 02 2262 8468

Adam et Rope Sendai

Architect: Tsutomu Kurokawa Photographer: © Kozo Takayama

The double-height window makes the shop more visible and fills the inside with daylight. Interior elements provide a dynamic rhythm to an otherwise excessively large space for selling clothes and complements.

Das Schaufenster doppelter Höhe macht das Geschäft sichtbar und lässt Tageslicht in den gesamten Raum fallen. Die Elemente im Inneren schaffen einen nervösen Rhythmus in einem Raum, der sonst zu groß und hoch für eine Boutique mit Kleidern und Accessoires wäre.

La devanture à double hauteur fait que la boutique est visible et inonde l'espace de lumière. Les éléments de l'intérieur créent un rythme dynamique dans un espace qui par ailleurs pourrait paraître trop grand et élevé pour une boutique de vêtements et d'accessoires.

El escaparate de doble altura hace la tienda visible y proporciona luz a todo el espacio. Los elementos del interior proporcionan un ritmo dinámico a un espacio que de otra manera parecería demasiado grande y alto para una tienda de ropa y complementos.

La vetrina con doppia altezza rende visibile il negozio e proporziona luce a tutto lo spazio. Gli elementi dell'interno danno un ritmo nervoso ad uno spazio che, in altro modo, sembrerebbe troppo grande ed alto per un negozio d'abbigliamento ed accessori.

Mariahilferstraße 49, 1060 Wien, Austria. Tel. +43 1 586 61 70
www.gil-area.com

Gil

Architect: Propeller Z **Photographer:** © Margherita Spiluttini

The color red, in combination with the remainder of the interior decoration, brings energy and move-ment to this anti-conventional shop interior, where a disorder and unfinished effect is desired. The lighting accentuates the color more deeply and makes this space, lacking in natural light, a gay and radiant place to be in.

Die Farbe Rot und die Dekoration im Inneren verleihen diesem Shop Energie und Dynamik, der sich in kein konventionelles Schema einordnen lässt und Ausdrucksformen sucht, die ungeordnet und halb fertig wirken. Die Beleuchtung unterstreicht die Farbe noch mehr und macht diese Räume, in die wenig Tageslicht fällt, heiter und lebhaft.

La couleur rouge, en plus de la décoration intérieure, confère énergie et dynamisme à une boutique qui s'écarte de tout conventionnalisme et cherche des formes hétéroclites à moitié achevées. L'éclairage accentue encore plus la couleur et transforme un espace dépourvu de lumière naturelle en un lieu emprunt de gaieté et de dynamisme.

El color rojo, junto con la decoración interior, imprime energía y dinamismo a una tienda que rehuye de cualquier convencionalismo y busca formas desordenadas y a medio construir. La iluminación acen-túa aún más el color y convierte un espacio sin mucha luz natural en un lugar alegre y dinámico.

Il color rosso, insieme all'arredamento interno, imprime energia e dinamismo ad un negozio che sfug-ge da qualsiasi convenzionalismo e cerca delle forme disordinate e costruite a metà. L'illuminazione accentua ancor di più il colore e trasforma uno spazio privo di molta luce naturale in un luogo allegro e dinamico.

Barcelona 4, Manresa, Spain Tel. +34 938 748 108

www.sitamurt.com

Sita Murt

Architect: Manuel Bailo i Rosa Rull **Photographer:** © Jordi Miralles

Sita Murt

Gil

Adam et Rope Sendai

Pinceau

Custo Barcelona / Sevilla

Ras Gallery

Custo Barcelona / Tokyo

Miss Sixty / Energie

Parafarmacia

Issey Miyake

Marni

   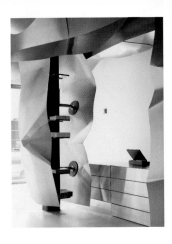

Deconstruction

Attualmente le grandi marche offrono, più che un prodotto, uno stile di vita specifico, ecco dunque che la loro immagine corporativa è sempre più importante. Le campagne pubblicitarie mostrano il comportamento di personaggi in un ambiente in cui gli articoli sono relegati ad un secondo piano, ed allora i negozi devono trasmettere lo stile di vita della marca ma potenziando al massimo, allo stesso tempo, gli oggetti in vendita. Per questo i negozi sono degli spazi sempre più eterogenei e diversi, ed ogni giorno nascono nuove tendenze e funzioni. Pur così, vi è una serie di stili dominanti che, sebbene spesso si mescolano tra loro, sono sufficientemente potenti da lasciar lo spazio a questa necessità di mostrare uno stile di vita più che un oggetto.

Trent'anni dopo il suo avvento, il minimalismo continua ad essere uno degli stili più presenti nel mondo dell'abbigliamento e del design. Le superfici bianche ed i campionari ordinati costituiscono un fondo neutro perfetto che fa risaltare la merce, trasmettendo eleganza e qualità. Più o meno simili sono le qualità dello stile classico moderno, in cui l'ordine va accompagnato da materiali ricchi e da mobili di design che creano atmosfere di lusso e comfort, cosa che lo rende uno degli stili preferiti dalle grandi marche. Invece, il "trash-chic" trae le sue radici dal "punk" ed abbina il design alla novità con materiali semplici e riciclati. Questa tendenza influisce sempre di più sullo stile casual, dando un tocco stravagante all'estetica urbana, sino ad oggi, comoda e funzionale. Il deconstruttivismo, apparso alla fine degli anni ottanta nell'ambito dell'alta cultura, è oggigiorno uno degli stili dominanti per la sua immaginazione e grand'eloquenza, come pure le importanti messe in scena, sempre più comuni ed immaginative. La trasformazione degli spazi industriali o classici in negozi, ha creato uno stile proprio, molto apprezzato dai designer, come il design di uno spazio attraverso i colori, in voga dal boom della Pop Art sino agli anni settanta.

Actualmente las grandes marcas ofrecen, más que un producto, un estilo de vida concreto, por lo que su imagen corporativa es un aspecto cada vez más importante. Las campañas publicitarias muestran el comportamiento de unos personajes concretos en un decorado en el que los artículos quedan relegados a un segundo plano, de manera que las tiendas deben transmitir el estilo de vida de la marca pero a la vez potenciar al máximo los objetos que están a la venta. Por eso, las tiendas son espacios cada vez más heterogéneos y diversos, y cada día aparecen nuevas tendencias y funciones. Aun así, hay una serie de estilos dominantes que, a pesar de que a menudo se entremezclan, son suficientemente potentes como para dar cabida a esta necesidad de mostrar un estilo de vida más que un objeto concreto.

Treinta años después de su aparición, el minimalismo sigue siendo uno de los estilos más presentes en el mundo de la ropa y del diseño. Las superficies blancas y los muestrarios ordenados constituyen un fondo neutro perfecto que resalta las mercancías y transmite elegancia y calidad. Bastante parecidas son las cualidades del estilo clásico moderno, en el cual el orden va acompañado de materiales ricos y de mobiliario de diseño que crea atmósferas de lujo y confort, por lo que es uno de los estilos preferidos de las grandes marcas. Por el contrario, el "trash-chic" tiene sus raíces en el "punk" y combina el diseño y la novedad con materiales sencillos o reciclados. Esta tendencia influye cada vez más en el estilo casual y añade un toque extravagante a la estética urbana, hasta ahora cómoda y funcional. El deconstructivismo, que apareció a finales de los ochenta en el ámbito de la alta cultura, es hoy en día uno de los estilos dominantes por su imaginación y grandilocuencia, al igual que las grandes puestas en escena, cada vez más comunes e imaginativas. La transformación de espacios industriales o clásicos en tiendas ha generado un estilo propio, muy apreciado por los diseñadores, como el diseño de un espacio a través de los colores, en uso desde el estallido del Pop Art en los años sesenta.

A l'heure actuelle, les grandes marques offrent, plus qu'un produit, un style de vie concret, sublimant leur image de marque. Les campagnes publicitaires exaltent le comportement de personnages dans un décor où les articles sont relégués au second plan, laissant aux magasins la tâche de transmettre un style de vie proposé par la marque tout en maximalisant les objets mis en vente. Les boutiques deviennent ainsi des espaces de plus en plus hétérogènes et multiples, avec l'apparition quotidienne de nouvelles tendances et fonctions. Mais des grands styles prédominent encore, malgré un certain engouement pour les mélanges, parvenant à satisfaire cette nécessité de montrer un mode de vie plus qu'un objet.

Trente ans après son apparition, le minimalisme continue à régner en maître sur le monde de la couture et du design. Les surfaces blanches et les présentoirs ordonnés constituent une toile de fond neutre parfaite qui exalte le produit tout en déclinant élégance et qualité. Les caractéristiques du style classique moderne sont assez similaires, fort d'un agencement ordonné accompagné de matériaux riches et de mobilier design qui créent une atmosphère de luxe et de confort. C'est un des styles préférés des grandes marques. Par contre, le « trash-chic » est issu du « punk » et combine design et nouveauté à des matériaux simples ou recyclés. Cette tendance influe chaque jour davantage sur le style désinvolte apportant une touche d'extravagance à l'esthétique urbaine, davantage axée sur l'aspect pratique et fonctionnelle. Le déconstructivisme, qui fait son apparition à la fin des années quatre-vingt au sein du monde de la culture, est aujourd'hui un des styles qui préside par son imagination et sa grandiloquence, à l'instar des grandes mises en scène, toujours plus répandues et fantaisistes. La réhabilitation d'espaces industriels ou classiques en magasins a engendré un style unique, très prisé par les designers, à l'image du design de l'espace par le biais des couleurs, établit depuis l'explosion du Pop Art dans les années soixante.

Heutzutage bieten die großen Marken nicht nur ein Produkt an, sondern einen konkreten Lebensstil. Deshalb wird ihr Corporate Image auch immer wichtiger. Die Werbekampagnen zeigen das Verhalten von einigen Personen innerhalb einer Umgebung und vor einer Dekoration, in der die Artikel den Hintergrund einnehmen. Die Verkaufslokale müssen also den Lebensstil der Marke vermitteln, aber gleichzeitig die Objekte, die verkauft werden sollen, maximal fördern. Deshalb werden Geschäfte in der heutigen Zeit immer vielgestaltiger und unterschiedlicher, und jeden Tag tauchen neue Trends und Funktionen auf. Dennoch gibt es eine Reihe von dominanten Stilen, die oft miteinander vermischt werden und die ausdrucksvoll genug sind, um die Anforderung, eher einen Lebensstil zu zeigen als einfach nur ein Objekt, zu erfüllen.

Noch dreißig Jahre nach seinem Auftauchen ist der Minimalismus weiterhin eine der Stilrichtungen, die am häufigsten in der Welt der Kleidung und des Designs anzutreffen ist. Weiße Flächen und geordnete Ausstellungselemente stellen den perfekten neutralen Hintergrund dar, um die Waren hervorzuheben und Eleganz und Qualität zu vermitteln. Der Stil der klassischen Moderne ist dem Minimalismus sehr ähnlich. Hier wird die Ordnung von edlen Materialien und Designermöbeln begleitet, so dass eine Atmosphäre von Luxus und Komfort entsteht. Das macht ihn zu einem der beliebtesten Stile bei den großen Marken. Im Gegensatz dazu hat der „Trash-Chic" seinen Ursprung in der Punkbewegung und kombiniert Design mit neuen einfachen und recycelten Materialien. Diese Tendenz ist immer häufiger bei dem so genannten Casual-Stil anzutreffen, der der urbanen Ästhetik, die bisher bequem und funktionell war, einen Touch von Extravaganz verleiht. Der Dekonstruktivismus, der gegen Ende der Achtzigerjahre des vergangenen Jahrhunderts im gehobenen Kulturbereich auftauchte, ist heute aufgrund seines Einfallsreichtums und seiner Abgehobenheit einer der dominanten Stile. Er gleicht großen Inszenierungen, die immer häufiger und einfallsreicher werden. Durch die Umformung von industriellen oder klassischen Räumen in Geschäfte ist ein eigener Stil entstanden, der von den Innenarchitekten sehr geschätzt wird, ebenso wie die Gestaltung eines Raumes durch die Farben, die seit dem Aufkommen der Pop-Art in den Sechzigerjahren angewandt wird.

Today's leading brand names are more than just a product; they signify an entire life style. Corporate image is becoming increasingly essential. Advertising campaigns present people inside a stylised décor, within which the commodities are secondary features. Shopping sites must suggest these lifestyle environments inside which they exhibit the merchandise with maximum appeal. As a result, shops and stores are becoming more diverse and heterogeneous spaces where new trends and tendencies appear every day. By and large there are a number of generic, prevailing styles which can be intermingled and are sufficiently suggestive to facilitate the portrayal of a way of life rather than a mere object of desire.

Thirty years after its introduction, Minimalism continues to be one of the principal styles in the world of clothing and design. Clear surfaces and arranged displays provide the ideal neutral setting to showcase the merchandise whilst suggesting elegance and quality. Classic modern style resembles minimalism, it combines rich materials with designer furnishings and a sense of order to create a lavish and comfortable feel. This is one of the preferred styles with the big brand names. In contrast to this, "trash-chic" has its roots in punk and combines inventive design with new-look, whilst using simple or recycled materials. This trend is increasingly influencing popular casual styles as it lends a touch of extravagance to urban aesthetics, which until now had been utilitarian and matter-of-fact. Deconstructionism, which appeared around the end of the 1980s within the high culture sphere, is today a leading style due to its imaginativeness and "high-flying" appeal, in a similar way to grandiose mise-en-scènes, which are also becoming more frequent and creative. Likewise, the transformation of industrial or long-established locales into new retail venues has created another innovative style, popular among designers as is the design of space through color, in evidence since the explosion of Pop Art in the 1960s.

Contemporary Classic

Trash-Chic

Mise-en-scène

Urban

278 King's Road, London SW3 5AW, U.K. Tel. +44 20 7368 7600
www.poliform.it

Poliform

Architect: George Khachfe **Photographer:** © Roger Casas

The two-storey premises allows very distinctive spaces to be created and, at the same time, permit sufficient space for the furniture to be displayed individually. The soberness of the shop is also reflected in the furniture.

Die doppelte Höhe des Raumes machte es möglich, sehr verschiedene Räume zu gestalten und gleichzeitig hatte man genug Platz, um die Möbel auszustellen, ohne sie miteinander zu mischen. Die Schlichtheit des Shops entspricht auch den Möbeln.

La double hauteur de la boutique engendre des espaces très divers tout en permettant que les meubles exposés aient suffisamment d'espace pour qu'ils ne se mêlent pas entre eux. La sobriété de la boutique se reflète sur les meubles.

La doble altura de la tienda permite crear espacios muy distintos y, al mismo tiempo, que los muebles expuestos tengan espacio suficiente para que no se mezclen entre ellos. La sobriedad de la tienda se transmite también a sus muebles.

La doppia altezza del negozio consente di creare spazi molto diversi e, allo stesso tempo, permette ai mobili esposti di non mischiarsi tra di loro. La sobrietà del negozio si trasmette anche ai suoi mobili.

Valencia 1, 08015 Barcelona, Spain Tel. +34 932 260 676
www.pilma.com

Pilma

Architect: Eduardo Samsó **Photographer:** © Jordi Miralles

The wooden staircase makes a statement in this shop. It is the centerpiece and is the only feature that remains the same through the changing seasons, unlike the rest of the decoration. Wood is also used on the counter and for the first floor ceilings.

Die Holztreppe verleiht dem Lokal Persönlichkeit und ist zugleich das einzige Element, das nicht in jeder Saison geändert wird so wie die übrige Dekoration. Auch der Verkaufstisch und die Decken im zweiten Stock sind mit Holz verkleidet.

L'escalier de bois qui donne du caractère à la boutique en est l'élément emblématique, car c'est le seul qui ne change pas au fil des saisons, contrairement au reste de la décoration. Le bois est également utilisé pour le comptoir et au plafond du deuxième étage.

La escalera de madera imprime personalidad a la tienda y es su elemento emblemático, ya que es el único que no cambia cada temporada, como el resto de la decoración. La madera también se utiliza en el mostrador y en los techos del segundo piso.

La scala di legno imprime personalità al negozio ed è il suo elemento emblematico, visto che è l'unico a non cambiare ogni stagione, come il resto dell'arredamento. Il legno è usato anche sul banco e sui soffitti del secondo piano.

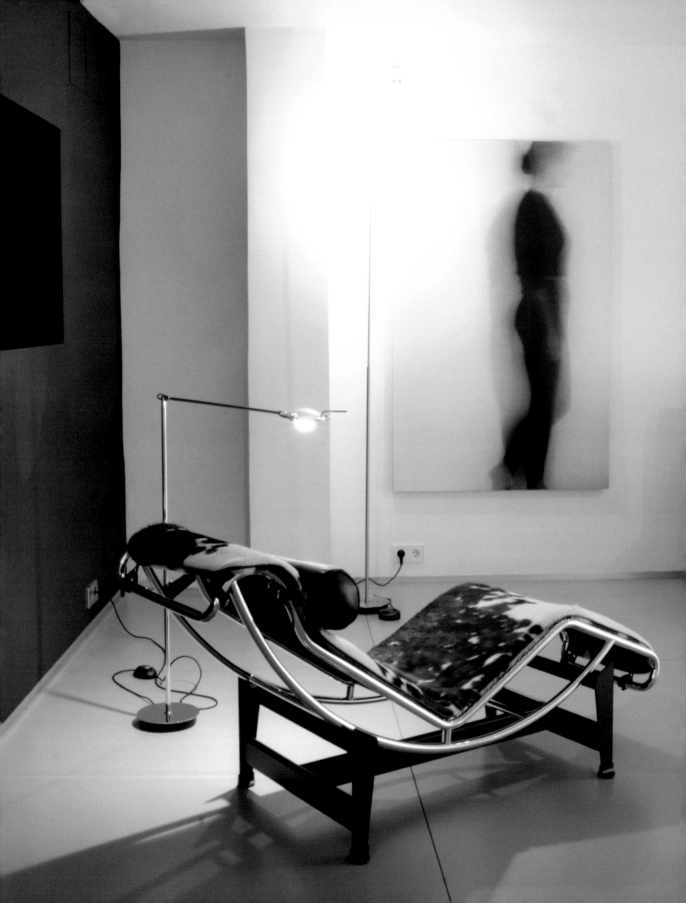

Rubinstein 4, 08022 Barcelona, Spain Tel. +34 934 189 550

www.greekbcn.com

Greek

Architect: Equipo Greek **Photographer:** © Alejandro Bachrach

Natural light floods the entire shop through the large windows stretching from the basement to the ground floor which reveal both levels to view from the street. Dining and kitchen spaces are displayed without clutter, stressing the elegant and leisurely flavor of these designs.

Durch die Schaufenster fällt Tageslicht in das gesamte Verkaufslokal, dank ihrer Höhe, die vom Untergeschoss bis zum Erdgeschoss reicht. So kann man beide Stockwerke von der Straße aus sehen. Die verschiedenen Vorschläge für Speisezimmer und Küchen werden ausgestellt, ohne dass der Raum zu überladen wird, denn der typische Zug dieser Einrichtungen ist die Klarheit und Eleganz des Designs.

Les devantures inondent de lumière naturelle toute la boutique grâce à la double hauteur entre le sous-sol et l'étage principal, de sorte que les deux étages sont visibles depuis la rue. Les différents modèles de salles à manger ou de cuisines sont exposés sans surcharger l'espace, car l'un des traits caractéristiques de cette ligne est la clarté et l'élégance de ses designs.

Los escaparates proporcionan luz natural a toda la tienda gracias a la doble altura entre el sótano y el piso principal, de manera que ambos pisos se pueden ver desde la calle. Las distintas propuestas de comedores o cocinas se exhiben sin sobrecargar el espacio, ya que uno de los rasgos distintivos de este equipo es la claridad y elegancia de sus diseños.

Le vetrine forniscono luce naturale a tutto il negozio grazie alla doppia altezza tra il piano interrato ed il piano principale, in modo che i due piani sono visibili dalla strada. Le varie proposte di saloni o cucine sono esposte senza caricare troppo lo spazio, giacché uno degli elementi distintivi di questa casa è la luminosità e l'eleganza dei suoi disegni.

10 Egret Way, Mill Valley, CA 94941, USA Tel. +1 415 388 8780

Kode

Architect: Studio o+a **Photographer:** © David Wakely

The brand's logo is used as another decorative element, and is present on all the walls and even on the floor. The constant presence of the logo and the scant furnishings provide a youthful, relaxed atmosphere suited to the targeted customers.

Das Markenlogo wurde als ein weiteres Dekorationselement eingesetzt, deshalb ist es überall an den Wänden und sogar auf dem Boden zu finden. Durch die ständige Präsenz des Logos und die wenigen Möbel entsteht eine lockere und jugendliche Atmosphäre, gut geeignet für die Kundschaft, auf die diese Marke hinzielt.

Le logo de la marque est utilisé comme si c'était un élément décoratif supplémentaire, ce qui explique sa présence sur tous les murs et même sur le sol. L'omniprésence de ce logo et le minimum de mobilier parviennent à créer une ambiance décontractée et jeune qui s'adresse à la clientèle de la marque.

El logotipo de la marca está utilizado como si fuera un elemento decorativo más, por lo que está presente en todos los muros e incluso en el suelo. Con la constante presencia del logotipo y el escaso mobiliario se consigue crear un ambiente desenfadado y juvenil, que es el tipo de público al que se dirige la marca.

Il logo della marca è usato come se fosse un elemento decorativo in più, ed è dunque presente su tutti i muri ed addirittura sul pavimento. Con la costante presenza del logo e gli scarsi mobili, si riesce a creare un ambiente rilassato e giovanile che è il tipo di pubblico al quale si rivolge la marca.

2-2-5 Oote Matsumoto-shi, Nagano-ken, Tokyo, Japan

La Ciénaga

Architect: Hideo Yasui **Photographer:** © Nacàsa & Partners

Although the entrance is set off from the street, this spectacular facade lures the customer inside. The ramps and steps crossing this neutral space do not rob it of its clear-cut lines, since they are constructed of light materials which do not obstruct the passage of light.

Obwohl der Eingang dieses Geschäfts von der Straßenlinie zurückgesetzt ist, wirkt seine auffallende Fassade als Reklame und als Vorplatz für den Innenraum. Rampen und Treppen durchqueren diesen minimalistischen und klaren Raum, ohne die Helligkeit zu beeinträchtigen, da sie aus leichten, lichtdurchlässigen Materialien sind.

Outre le fait que l'entrée de la boutique avance jusqu'au bord de la rue, sa façade spectaculaire sert de réclame et de préambule à l'intérieur. Les rampes et escaliers traversent un espace minimaliste et net sans en réduire la clarté, étant construits à base de matériaux légers qui laissent passer la lumière.

A pesar de que la entrada de la tienda se retranquea con respecto a la línea de la calle, su espectacular fachada actúa como reclamo y preámbulo de su interior. Las rampas y escaleras atraviesan un espacio mínimo y limpio sin reducir la claridad, dado que están hechas de materiales poco pesados que dejan pasar la luz.

Pur se l'ingresso del negozio è collocato a squadra rispetto alla linea della strada, la sua spettacolare facciata agisce come richiamo e preambolo del suo interno. Le rampe e le scale attraversano uno spazio minimo e pulito senza ridurne la luce, perché fatte di materiali poco pesanti che lasciano passare la luce.

7407 Melrose Avenue, Los Angeles, CA 90046, USA Tel. +1 323 653 8255
www.laeyeworks.com

l.a. Eyeworks

Architect: Neil Denari Architects Inc. **Photographer:** © Benny Chan

Futurism, in this case, is a useful resource for highlighting the presence of the glasses in the shop, despite being kept low-key. The dominant feature here are the pathways that have been designed to meet customer needs.

Der futuristische Stil ist in diesem Fall ein Mittel, um die Präsenz der Brillen in dem Shop zu unterstreichen, auch wenn er nur als Hintergrund eingesetzt wird. Was den Raum wirklich beherrscht, sind die Wege, die so angelegt sind, dass sie den Bedürfnissen und Ansprüchen des Kunden entgegenkommen.

Dans ce cas particulier, le recours au style futuriste permet de mettre en valeur les lunettes exposées dans la boutique, même si elles sont au second plan. Ce qui domine vraiment l'espace, ce sont les allées et venues du client dans cet univers créé spécialement pour faciliter et répondre à ses attentes.

El estilo futurista es en este caso un recurso que refuerza la presencia de las gafas de la tienda, aunque se mantiene en un segundo plano. Lo que verdaderamente domina el espacio son los recorridos del cliente dentro del espacio, creado especialmente para facilitar y atender sus necesidades.

Lo stile futurista è in questo caso un ricorso che rafforza la presenza degli occhiali del negozio, pur mantenendosi in un secondo piano. Quello che domina veramente lo spazio sono i percorsi interni del cliente dentro il negozio, creati in modo speciale per agevolare ed dar risposta alle sue necessità.

346, rue Saint-Honoré, 75001 Paris, France Tel. +33 1 53 45 82 22
www.faceaface-paris.com

Face à Face

Designer: Western Design **Photographer:** © Roger Casas

The solution for these premises was rather complicated by the fact that the floor space is very small and the shop occupies four stories. For this reason the vertical characteristics were emphasized. The ground floor was opened to the street and the staircase was located in the background behind the counter.

Es war nicht ganz einfach, dieses Geschäft zu gestalten, denn das Grundstück ist sehr klein und der Shop erstreckt sich über vier Stockwerke. Deshalb mussten die Funktionen über die Stockwerke verteilt werden. Dazu wurde das Erdgeschoss zur Straße hin geöffnet und im Hintergrund hinter dem Ladentisch eine Treppe angebracht.

L'agencement de cet espace n'était pas facile à résoudre, vu l'exiguïté du terrain et la répartition de la boutique sur quatre étages, nécessitant un développement en hauteur. A cet effet, le rez-de-chaussée a été ouvert sur la rue et l'escalier placé au deuxième plan, derrière le comptoir.

La solución para este espacio era un tanto complicada, ya que el solar es muy pequeño y la tienda ocupa cuatro pisos, por lo que era necesario un desarrollo en altura. Para ello se abrió la planta baja a la calle y se situó la escalera en un segundo término, tras el mostrador.

La soluzione di questo spazio era un po' complessa, poiché la superficie era molto piccola ed il negozio occupa quattro piani, bisognava dunque svilupparlo in altezza. Per farlo si è aperto il piano terra alla strada, situando la scala in un secondo piano, dietro il banco.